P9-CEM-361

THE
NON-RUNNER'S
BOOK

PREVIOUS BOOKS BY THE AUTHORS:

Get Out of My Way or I'll Kill You: A Guide to Self-Assertiveness

Skateboarding for Dollars

You Can Learn Punk Guitar

The Quick Weight-Gain Diet

The Zen of Microwave

Sex for Clones

Amy Carter of Georgia: A Political Biography

Tennis in the Third Reich

Inflation Can Be Fun

Have You Got Your Ears On, Jesus? (The CB Prayerbook)

The Sauerkraut Cookbook

Whip Me, Little Girl

Fads: How to Spot Them, How to Turn a Quick Profit

THE
NON-RUNNER'S
BOOK

Vic Ziegel &
Lewis Grossberger

COLLIER BOOKS

A Division of Macmillan Publishing Co., Inc.

NEW YORK

Copyright © 1978 by Vic Ziegel and Lewis Grossberger

All rights reserved. No part of this book may be
reproduced or transmitted in any form or by any means,
electronic or mechanical, including photocopying,
recording or by any information storage and retrieval
system, without permission in writing from the Publisher.

Macmillan Publishing Co., Inc.
866 Third Avenue, New York, N.Y. 10022
Collier Macmillan Canada, Ltd.

Library of Congress Cataloging in Publication Data

Ziegel Vic.
    The non-runner's book.

    1. Jogging—Anecdotes, facetiae, satire, etc.
2. Running—Anecdotes, facetiae, satire, etc.
I. Grossberger, Lewis, joint author.   II. Title.
GV494.Z53   796.4′26   78-13069
ISBN 0-02-040920-6

Fourth Printing 1979

Designed by Jack Meserole

Printed in the United States of America

Dedicated to CALVIN COOLIDGE [1872-1933]
30th president of the United States

"I do not choose to run."

"Attention to health is the greatest hindrance to life."
—PLATO

"In the long run, we are all dead."
—JOHN MAYNARD KEYNES

PICTURE CREDITS: Cynthia Johnson: pages 8, 32, 42, 72, 83, 96; New York Roadrunner's Club: 12; Salvador Dali, "Original Sin": 18 (top); Columbia Pictures Corp.: 34; Universal: 99; W. Morris: 44; American International Pictures: 101; S. Hano: 98; Lew Grossberger: 78; New York Public Library: v, 13, 16, 18 (bottom), 19, 22, 24, 52, 75, 86, 89, 93.

Contents

Foreword

BY FRANK FOOTER,
Champion Non-Runner

For me, non-running is life itself. I know that might sound strange to the uninitiated. But if you'd been non-running as long as I have, you'd understand. I learned to walk at the age of two, and by two and a half, I was tired of it and lying down again. I was a varsity non-runner all through high school, and in college I was already having frequent fainting spells. Today I feel as tired as I did when I was a teenager, and though I'm forty-six, I haven't speeded up a bit. My doctor assures me I can go on like this for years and I'm eagerly awaiting old age and death.

Nowadays a lot of other people have begun to discover non-running. I see them from my bedroom window, where I have a telescope set up. I think it's terrific that so many newcomers are getting pleasure out of it. But still, I have to ask: Where were they back when I was out on a limb by myself? It makes me mad when I think about all the times I was ridiculed and ostracized for having the courage of my convictions. So don't be surprised if some time you come by my place and say, "Hey, Frank, I'm a non-runner too. How about let's go out and have a beer on me—whaddaya say, pal?" and I spit right in your eye and tell you to stick it. Because I've always been a guy who carries a grudge.

Introduction:

Ease on Off the Road

We are in the middle of a revolution. Suddenly, Americans by the millions—gaunt, out of breath, sorelegged—are casting off their costly and fetid sneakers and dropping by the wayside where they lie down, close their eyes, and smile broadly.

They are busy discovering the most relaxing new trend to hit the nation since Prohibition ended: not running.

After months or years of strenuous overexertion, people are beginning to ask *why*. Why drive yourself to the point of exhaustion? Why pound your feet to bloody stumps? Why pretend pain is good for you? Why terrorize entire communities by thundering around the streets in massive, unruly, grunting herds?

Why run?

Instead, why not not run?

Today, non-running is America's slowest but steadiest-growing pastime. The Bureau of Sedentary Activity estimates that there are more than 180 million non-runners in the United

States. What kind of people are these non-runners? Who are these pathfinders bold enough to drop out of the faddish rat race? Are they weirdos? buffoons? sociopaths? naive sycophants? craven toadies? harmless eccentrics? perverts? trolls? Medicaid cheaters? brainwashed zombies? Red spies?

Not at all.

Surprisingly, non-runners are very much like you and me. They include people from every walk of life. And there are not only walkers. There are sitters, leaners, nappers, starers, procrastinators, TV-watchers, popsicle-lickers, readers, sneezers, yawners, teasers, stumblers, lechers, stamp collectors, static-electricity gatherers, and, of course, the totally immobile.

This amazingly versatile group comprises people of all ages, races, and sexes. Non-running is accessible to young and old, rich and fat, the famous as well as the depressed. Whether you're an android or an aborigine, you can take part. Or you can take all.

Many non-runners have been doing it all their lives. Others have only recently kicked the running habit to join the swelling ranks of the unrun. Together, these non-runners spend an estimated $665 billion annually on products totally unrelated to running in any way. Without them and their non-running-related expenditures, the U.S. economy would fold up in a minute.

But the economic gain from non-running is only part of the picture. There is also the spiritual side. Non-runners are linked by a common bond; they feel a kinship that expresses itself in innumerable ways. Non-runners will often wave to other non-runners they don't even know. Sometimes they will even invite them home to dinner and later go to bed with them.

And there is the well-known psychological lift that comes to non-runners. After the first half hour or so of not running, you become so elated by the realization that you are not out in the hot sun or in the rain pounding around a hard sidewalk or dusty track that you may find yourself uttering a restrained sigh. This indefinable sense of quiet satisfaction is one of the things that makes not running so pleasurable.

People find that once they start to not run, it's hard to stop. After just a small taste, the tyro non-runner finds his body demanding more and more until he is almost smiling with the sheer joy of not running. It is this "up" feeling that enables veteran non-runners to achieve the amazing feats about which you've undoubtedly read. These are the so-called marathnoners who have attained the peak of the non-running experience. Some of them are capable of going twenty-four hours a day without a single running step. Even more astonishing, there are those who, by combining non-running with meditation, have achieved a mental state in which they don't even *think* about running for months on end.

Still another source of non-running's appeal is the surpassing ease with which it may be performed. As Dr. George Shoeshine, author of *Non-Running and Non-Being: The Totality of the Whole*, has eloquently put it, "The essence of not running —indeed, the beauty of it, as it were—is in its utter simplicity, if you know what I mean."

Non-running is so easy that it can be enjoyed at any time in any place: in city parks; alongside (or in) rivers, lakes, inland seas and oceans; atop mountains or supermarket shelves; on couches; inside roll-top desks; in the bath; out in the back; or over the rainbow. In 1972, the Russian cosmonaut Yuri Yugarin reported completing ten minutes of weightless non-running in space during the flight of Soyuz 12. He said it made him feel high.

And non-running is cheap. Sweatsuits, netted shirts, jockstraps, and German sneakers are not needed by non-runners. You can non-run in your street clothes, your formal wear, or in the nude. (While it's true that there are some non-runners who prefer special racing-stripe pajamas and leisure suits and who enjoy arguing the merits of hard slippers vs. soft, these are in the minority.)

Non-running gives the overstructured and overdirected life a needed sense of freedom and purposelessness. Life is, as we now know, totally meaningless, and artificial attempts to find goals and erect structures (like setting records or winning races) are doomed to fail and disappoint, ultimately leading to irreversible depression. The quicker you realize this, the happier you will be.

But some people never understand. Competitive, compulsive, indigestive, they become obsessed with crossing finish lines and counting laps. They wallow in linear thought. They begin to see life as a race. They have become running addicts, lured by the powerful metaphor of the race, with its false promise of getting someplace. They lose sight of the importance of staying in one spot and not moving for long periods of time. And they pay a fearful price in terms of curdled brains and the unnecessary provocation of untold thousands of innocent dogs that are rudely transformed into snapping curs with a morbid desire to taste the human ankle.

Non-runners do not have these problems. They truly understand the beauty and power of slow. They respect the concept of Take It Easy. They reject the pseudo-adventure of the road. They do not traffic in traffic. They know that wisdom can't be rushed. They know how to relax. Theirs is the way of the turtle and the snail. Theirs is the spirit of the glacier. The spirit of Walk, Do Not Run; of Haste Makes Waste; of Stop; and Halt; and Yield Right of Way. Grass grows under their feet and it tickles and that's nice. Baby ducks are not frightened by their passing. They are non-runners. And they know it.

**THE
NON-RUNNER'S
BOOK**

1 Non-Running for Beginners

How can I start non-running? That's the question we are asked more and more often. Exactly how is it different from non-humming, gun-running, and Jim Bunning? Can anyone non-run, or does he need this book to show him how? Are there non-running tours? What if you are caught non-running with someone under sixteen? What color is non-running? Is there a sales tax on it? Will it cause cancer? Why haven't I seen non-running T-shirts? And are you sure it takes a hyphen? Why not just say "nonrunning?"

Our answer, every time, is "Whoa, whoa, not so fast!"

What you must keep in mind is that non-running isn't any more complicated than putting one foot behind the other. The beginning non-runner is hardly at a disadvantage when meeting a person who has been non-running for years. In fact, an even bigger problem is how to recognize such a person (in non-runners' lingo, they are termed "advanced non-runners"). There is no sure way. Dr. Chaim Dry, a pioneer in stationary medicine, insists that he can spot an advanced non-runner from a hundred yards away. (Up close, nothing works.)

3

But back to the beginner; if you're one, answer these questions: Did you ever fall down? Did you ever catch cold and decide to take the rest of the day off and go to bed? Did you ever feel like exercising—and then fight off the impulse? Have you ever refused to offer your seat to an old lady on the bus?

If you answered Yes to any of these questions, you can non-run. (If you answered No to all of them, you're lying.)

Honest to God. You really can. We ask you to trust us on this. Non-running is a little like a religion. It requires an act of faith.

So get out there and get ready to get set.

WARMING DOWN

First, get your non-running clothes on (see chapter 3) and you're ready to st— Hold it! Don't start yet! It's important to be sure that your mind and body are prepared (non-running may draw on either). If people who are used to constant strenuous activity and exertion stop moving too soon, they could suffer immediate boredom and depression. Say a man has been working hard all day making sandwiches at a delicatessen counter and sprinting around the park at lunch. If he were to suddenly flop down on a couch for a long nap, he could be in serious trouble. His mind could go right on slicing tongue at top speed; his heart could go on beating at a machine-gun rate. The effect would be *just as if he weren't non-running at all*. Frightening.

This is why we feel warming down is so important. Of course, there are non-runners who think that warming down is not at all important. We don't agree. This is just one of the many spirited controversies connected with non-running that make it the exciting pastime that it is.

Anyway, here are a few basic warming-down exercises to get you started (these are not be confused with the basic Staying-Out-of-Shape Exercises covered in chapter 4).

To prepare your mind for non-running, let your head down slowly to the floor. Rub your forehead against the rug until static electricity builds up. Touch metal to discharge it. Repeat ten times or until you begin to smoke.

To prepare your body: Stand with feet together. Revolve slowly with your eyes closed while chanting "St. Louis Blues." After about two minutes, you should feel you've unwound. Now cross your legs and sit down. This relaxes the knee muscles. Next do the Eagle Rock with style and grace. Sway to the left, sway to the right. Stand up, sit down, fight, fight, fight. That's about it, really.

WHAT KIND OF CONDITION IS YOUR CONDITION IN?

Okay, you've got your non-running clothes on and you've warmed down and you're ready to start. Hold it! You're still not ready to start! Not until you've had a stretch test. No one, especially those under forty, should begin non-running until he or she has been to a physician or plumber for a complete checkout of physical fatness.

You see, a regular non-running program may place the body under great strain—particularly the stomach muscles, which may have to stretch considerably to accommodate the large amounts of food and drink taken in by non-runners. Likewise, the eye muscles of the typically athletic American may not be strong enough to handle the vast amount of reading, TV-watching, Pong-playing, and staring into the middle distance to which a non-runner's optic nerves are subjected. Also, a lightly used spine may rebel at the staunch support required of it by long hours of napping and resting.

People who have been running for a long time (in the jargon, they're termed "runners") are especially subject to health problems when they embark on a non-running program. They are so used to being wracked with constant pain that the sudden absence of it brought on by non-running often sends them into emotional tailspins that can have serious consequences, not only for them, but for all of society. For instance, a forty-six-year-old runner in Alabama who went cold turkey last winter picked up a loaded shotgun one day and, according to state police—

but, no, the case was much too gruesome for a book like this. Suffice it to say that veteran runners beginning to non-run seriously should consider seeing a reputable psychoanalyst or encounter group. Just to be on the safe side.

WHERE DO YOU NON-RUN TO?

Okay, you've got your non-running clothes on and you've warmed down and your stretch-test results have come back positive and you're ready to start. Got your license? Just kidding; you don't really need a license to non-run. Okay, go! What are you waiting for? Why are you still reading this? Do it. Get out there. But where? you ask. Anywhere, that's where. Inside, outside. But won't I feel stupid at first? you want to know. Won't people laugh at me? Of course they will. So what? Ignore them. Look, you're starting to get us mad now. Quit putting this off!

If you're really self-conscious, you can hail a taxi and start non-running in the back seat. Most drivers are too courteous to stare. Order him around the park. Cars in general are excellent non-running areas. A friend of ours, Miles Shmendrick, the used-car and citrus king ("See us if you want a lemon"), remembers the day he began non-running. "I remember the second day too," he recalls. "For after that, I've got to look at my diary."

Many non-runners keep diaries. Keeping a diary is a good idea. On really bad days it provides evidence that you exist. Miles showed us his diary once. He pulled out a huge sheet of figures with the date and place of each non-run. One entry caught our eye: "Dover Garage, '75 Ford, back seat, five hrs, unsuccessful." We asked Miles to explain.

"I had just lost a major business deal and I thought my company would be wiped out," he said.

"So to relax your shattered nerves, you needed five hours of non-running, right?"

"No, not quite," said Miles. "That five hours in the back seat was a suicide attempt. Windows closed, motor running, potato over the exhaust pipe. The 'unsuccessful' means I wasn't successful."

"How come?"

"I was using one of my own cars."

DO IT YOUR WAY

Remember when you learned how to read in grade school and you had to memorize the alphabet in exactly the correct order? Every damn letter right where it belonged? And remember how, when you were in marine boot camp, you had to hold the rifle exactly the way the drill instructor ordered you to or he'd bury you up to your neck in an anthill? Well, non-running isn't like that.

No, sir. Non-running is the most natural thing there is. Every non-runner has his own style and nobody can tell you that style is wrong. You can non-run on your head if you want to, and not even the U. S. Supreme Court could declare it an illegal non-run. (In fact, three of the Supreme Court justices habitually deliver their opinions sitting on their heads, though this is a carefully kept secret.)

Never try to imitate anyone else's non-running style. (Especially ours, which has been copyrighted. We see anybody imitating our style, we get really steamed.) There are, however, a couple of points to remember about style: Keep your body straight, your head down, and your nose bent. Always keep the knees closed and the eyes slightly open. Lock your wrists, flex your biceps, flatten your tendons, and put your left foot slightly in front of your right. Your toes should be relaxed and your fists clenched, but calm. Your lip should be curled. If you have a mustache, cover it with your tongue. If this feels difficult at first, pull the tongue out manually with your left hand. Keep both shoulders crossed. Take quick, shallow, rasping breaths. Swallow frequently and keep the lips moist. Count to yourself and blink on numbers divisible by ten. Keep your hat on. Keep your nose clean. Make sure you go to the bathroom before starting. Just be completely natural and do whatever *you* like. Remember, non-running shouldn't be work. It's to enjoy!

RIGHT

How to apply non-running principles to achieve successful park-bench use.

WRONG

HOW MUCH NON-RUNNING TO START?

Not too much! That's the best advice we can give. Bad things can happen to wise guys who think they're such big shots they can just step out as fine as you please on their first day of non-running and go like a champ. For heaven's sake, take it easy. There's nothing to prove, so try to act like an adult. (Children should not be reading this book. They should be reading our earlier work, *Non-Running for the Temporarily Small.*)

Remember what happened to R. V. Winkle of upstate New York who tried for a marathon nap without working up to it gradually. A classic case of rest slippage ensued and Winkle wound up in four medical textbooks and a nonfiction novel. His beard went on tour with P. T. Barnum for sixteen smash weeks, then ran off with Jenny Lind, the Swedish Nightingale, who used to nest in it.

Listen to your body. It knows what's good for you, although sometimes it's too mean to tell. Bodies are secretive by nature. Non-run for fifteen minutes or so and then put your ear to your body. If the body says nothing, non-run a bit more. If the body groans, rumbles, squeaks, or makes even less refined protests, come back tomorrow. Otherwise you could end up a nobody.

WHAT IF I GET SORE?

Hey, don't get sore. Nobody likes a sorehead. Some soreness may be inevitable at first. After all, you're asking your mind and body to adjust to a whole new way of life and nobody likes to make changes. So it's possible you may get somewhat sore or glum or crabby or cranky, or Sleepy or Sneezy. This shouldn't last long. If it does, see your doctor. Or see our doctor. If he asks about us, tell him the check is in the mail.

DO I NEED A TV SET?

This is an individual decision. Some non-runners swear by TV, while others swear at it. We personally have found that

TV can be helpful, especially for beginners who are having trouble finding their individual non-running metier.

Here's one of the simplest methods we know to begin non-running: Watch an afternoon quiz show. You will find yourself naturally dropping into the position the French call *Le Poisson Froid.* Soon you'll find yourself non-running with no effort at all. During commercials you may take breaks and do your warming-down exercises.

Be careful, however, not to accidentally turn on a soap opera. Too often, viewers become attached to the characters and begin thinking of them as friends and members of the family. If this happens to you, you may lose your concentration on non-running and soon find it slipping away into the background. Your form will suffer as you wonder if kindly avocado farmer Joe Arnold will discover that his fiancée, Mary Jane Donaldson, before her mysterious operation, played left tackle for the Chicago Bears.

With quiz shows there is absolutely no danger of ever identifying with anyone involved.

Once you've become accustomed to TV non-running, you may wish to try a more advanced activity: non-TV non-running.

Start by turning off the set. This may require great willpower. At first you may feel uncomfortable non-running without hearing people choosing categories, making deals, or jumping up and down ecstatically. Don't be alarmed. Many non-runners before you have overcome that hurdle.

We're not going to kid you and tell you it's easy. You may be tempted to shout out several of Tony Randall's most cherished clues from "The $10,000 Pyramid" or Paul Lynde ad libs from "Hollywood Squares." That's perfectly okay. Sooner or later, your neighbors will help you kick that habit. Especially if your walls are as thin as ours.

Then, finally, you'll be non-running for the pure, unalloyed joy of it. Longer and longer you'll non-run, the air pollution whistling freely through your pores. In front of color consoles, black-and-whites, Betamaxes, and Cuisinarts. Off they go and on you go, non-running up a storm. You'll know you're improving when you see your electricity bill.

2

How to Avoid the Boston Marathon

THE MARATHON TRADITION

The first marathon run came about in this way. In 490 B.C., the Persians invaded Greece. The Greeks did not care for this. A force of 10,000 angry Athenians, though outnumbered six to one, triumphed over the Persians in a battle on the plain of Marathon. They killed about 6,400 Persians and drove the invaders back to their ships.

The news of the victory was entrusted to a courier, who was sent racing to Athens, nearly 23 miles away. There is some question as to his identity. Some historians give the name as Phillippides or Pheidippides, though others argue that point. All agree on one thing though: Somebody ran the news back to Athens. According to reliable sources, he said upon arrival, "Rejoice, we conquer!" Then he dropped dead.

This is the great tradition that modern marathon racers seek to emulate.

On the third Monday in April all eyes turn to Boston, which is not too surprising, since those eyes get a chance to focus on several thousand people wearing nothing more than numbers and underwear.

The non-runner, of course, is always prepared for the Boston Marathon. Some of us take the green-and-white pill developed by Dr. Zoltan Foxtrot. The pill deadens for forty-eight hours that area of the brain which receives the news reports from northeastern states. (Unfortunately, there are side effects. One non-runner who took the pill didn't get any news from as far north as Labrador for eight years.)

11

The National Federation of Non-Runners is making this photo available to all its members as a precaution. Any one of these marathoners may some day move into your neighborhood or try to marry your sister or ask to borrow your comb. Study the picture; learn the faces and numbers. Just because you're a non-runner doesn't mean you have to take it lying down.

In the early 1930s, running was unpopular, and in many areas, runners were attacked by howling mobs. As a result, running togs were designed to protect the wearer. In this 1937 photo, Olympic miler Basil Belknap of Cincinnati takes a practice run, wearing a gray, three-button worsted warm-up suit, white-buck running shoes, and a gray, snap-brim headband.

Dr. Foxtrot is currently at work on a pill that will isolate Boston and the immediate suburbs. At present, he has a blue-and-yellow capsule that rejects news from Newton and Natick and the lobby bar in the Ritz-Carlton. Bravo, doctor.

The inexperienced non-runner will think we are needlessly concerned and he may be right. But we don't believe so. (And we wrote the book.)

To prove our point, we retell the story of Archie LeStoil, a non-runner who thought he could avoid news of the marathon by retreating to the wood-paneled interior of his neighborhood pub, the Rack and Thumbscrew. He was on his second drink when three strangers stepped into the bar. They were very excited, and although the bartender asked them to keep their voices down, Archie couldn't help hearing some of their conversation.

The tallest of the three said something that sounded like "Blah blah blah Frank Shorter, blah blah blah second place, blah blah . . . "

This drew a heated reply of "Blah blah blah finish line, blah blah blah, Japan, Australia, blah blah Heartbreak Hill, blah blah . . . "

The third party broke his silence with "Blah, two hours, blah minutes, blah blah record, blah blah new books, blah blah . . . "

Archie left. "I was still shaking when I got home," he said. "It got even worse when I saw my son. He had a bloody nose and his non-running T-shirt was torn and he was crying pretty hard for someone thirty years old."

"Dad," Archie's son said, "a lot of the other kids started running after me and yelling nasty things. Dad, is it true that we don't have any running books in the house?"

Archie told him that was true.

"And, Dad, they said you don't own a pair of running shoes."

"We have lots of other shoes, Son. Just the other day I bought a pair of caterpillar slippers—"

"It's not the same thing, Dad. All the other kids talk about how far their fathers run and I never know what to say. And the other guys made fun of me because they said you took a little pill that blanked out all the news from the Boston Marathon."

That was too much for Archie. "It's a damned lie," he shouted. "I never took that pill in my life. You tell your rotten friends that I spend marathon day in the Rack and Thumbscrew. I do my best to get stinko and blot everything out. Don't you remember last year when the cops brought me home after I passed out on the endives at Tony's Market?"

The tears were beginning to slow down. "I—I think so—"

"Son," Archie said, "there's a lot of people in this world who think their way is right because they read about it in a bestselling book. My policy has always been to live and let live. The other fellow is entitled to make an ass of himself in shorts and sneakers and I expect him to let me do the same thing right here on my couch in front of the television set."

We're proud of Archie. And all you terrific moms and dads out there who have found other ways to avoid the Boston Marathon. Especially our non-running friends in the Boston area who really have a problem, come marathon day.

Most of them leave town, taking whatever possessions their flabby arms and legs enable them to carry. Others get sick and throw up. Still others hide behind their accent. Carl Yastrzemski plays baseball. If you have a favorite method, why not share it with our Boston friends? Remember, someday there might be a marathon through the streets of your city. We can't all be lucky enough to live in Venice.

3

Stuff

One of the best things about non-running is that it requires so little in the way of clothing and equipment,

Follies dancer Fifi LaZetz shocked all of France in 1912 when she insisted on non-running in the nude in a lace-covered bucket. Fifi's mother (right) came to her defense. And read her the funnies, too.

or "stuff," as it is termed in non-running slang. Non-runners are notoriously individualistic and no two look alike.

You can dress either as expensively or cheaply as your budget and conscience allow. The main principle to follow is this: Start from the inside and work your way out. Nothing is more frustrating than putting on your coat or trousers only to realize that your underwear is still in the drawer where you left it.

The question of nude non-running seems to come up these days whenever non-runners gather. Of course, it is still illegal in many areas but seems to be slowly gaining acceptance. Some cities and localities have set aside special areas where the unabashed may shed their clothing and non-run to their hearts' content—as long as they don't touch. Once touching begins, it can spread like wildfire. Buckets of ice-cold water and hoses are usually kept handy in these areas to cope with any problems that arise.

But enough of generalities. Here are some specific answers to some of the most commonly asked questions about "stuff."

SHOES

Get a shoe. Right now. Go out and get a shoe. In fact, get two. A good pair of non-running shoes protects the foot from reality, shielding it from any emotional shocks and ugly rumors.

If a shoe sees you coming and runs away, you'll know it's a running shoe and not a non-running shoe. Let it go. Non-running shoes are specially built to take the kind of punishment that serious non-running can dish out.

A few years ago, most non-running shoes were made of Dacron polyester. Now almost all of the reputable brands are of imitation wood, which is more solid and can be nailed to the floor for total stability. These shoes require a breaking-in period. About three years ought to suffice. Maintenance is simple. If they get dirty, clean them with some sandpaper and varnish.

Try on all shoes before buying. Take your time. Test them if you can. See how they fit lying down, sitting, having sex. If they're so tight that you find yourself screaming in pain, try

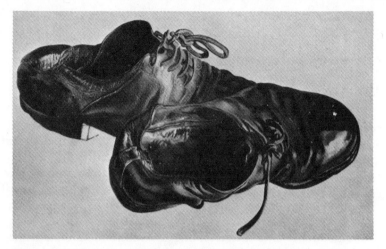

First pair of non-running shoes, built by the semi-legendary Azi Zucker, founder of the Azusa shoe empire. Azi was a starving young shoeshine boy in Düsseldorf in 1947 when he made this prototype pair out of discarded GI boots. Upon finishing them, Azi growled at the shoes, then attacked them with a lead pipe, but they did not run away. "Ven I seen dat, I knew I was in, baby," Azi later wrote in his all-dialect autobiography, No Biz Like Shoe Biz.

This famous door in Düsseldorf, Germany, is the barn door through which the young and lonely Azi Zucker was kicked by an enraged farmer who had discovered him telling off-color stories to underage heifers. The kick, which left a permanent imprint in Zucker's left buttock, inspired him to build his first pair of non-running shoes, leading directly to the foundation of the great Azusa shoe empire.

OPPOSITE: Azi Zucker, founder and president of the giant Azusa Shoe Corporation, still insists on personally testing each new model, despite phenomenal growth of his concern, now producing 450 new non-running styles a day, plus laces. Here Zucker tries a test melody after donning new Azusa Yodeler SL600s, specially designed for nighttime wear by Swiss goatherds. Zucker found his pitch too low, sent shoes back to drawing board with orders to engineers to tighten shoe.

Table 1   A Practical Guide to Non-Running Shoes

SHOE	PRIMARY USE	SOAKING
Azusa XL 1200s	The all-purpose shoe	•
Pima Colada	Sunday drinking	•
Nuke Waffle Trainer	Eating breakfast	
Azusa Cucamongas	Tourism	
Nookie SX1400s	Visiting singles bars	
Ah-Doo-Dah Clopper	Day at the races	•
New Ballast Hangarounds	Loitering	
FootKing Groaners	Moping	•
Needle Sniffers	Doping	
Logical Positivist 380s	Hoping	
Inter Loafers	Voyeurism	
Moaning Whiner	Sulking	
Hoohah Hoofers	Cruising	
U.S. Kegs	Boozing	•
Coma Slippers	Snoozing	
Azusa Cortexes	Perusing	
Jaws Cruncher	Bathing	•
Nerd '50s	Hair-combing	
Thom McCheap Snazzies	Trying on shoes	
RCA Victims	Listening to records	
Achilles Tendencies	Healing	
Nose Clogs	Catching cold	•
Feetnik Sandals	Reading poetry to jazz	
Pius XVIIIs	Papal audiences	
Skin Simulators	Going barefoot	•

the next size. Beware the advice of unscrupulous shoe salesmen. And at all costs, be sure to bring with you the following guide:

THE FOLLOWING GUIDE

Finding the right shoe is vital, no matter what your choice of non-running activity. So is finding the left shoe. Fortunately, there has been a vast growth in the number and style of non-

SITTING	SMOKING	WAITING	FALLING	DESPAIR
•	•	•	•	•
	•		•	
				•
	•	•		
•				•
		•		
•		•		•
	•		•	
		•		
•			•	
		•		•
•		•		
•				•
	•			
	•	•		•
				•
•	•	•		
•		•		
			•	

running shoes available. In the last week alone, six hundred new shoes hit the market. The market went to one knee and took an eight count.

We have studied, analyzed, and personally tested every non-running shoe made (with the exception of Size −2, recommended for the eight-month fetus). We can attest from personal experience that there's a non-running shoe for whatever activity you engage in. For our recommendations, see Table 1.

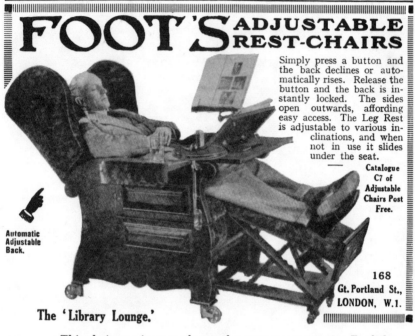

FOOT'S ADJUSTABLE REST-CHAIRS

Simply press a button and the back declines or automatically rises. Release the button and the back is instantly locked. The sides open outwards, affording easy access. The Leg Rest is adjustable to various inclinations, and when not in use it slides under the seat.

Catalogue C7 of Adjustable Chairs Post Free.

Automatic Adjustable Back.

168 Gt. Portland St., LONDON, W.1.

The 'Library Lounge.'

This chair was immensely popular among non-running Englishmen of the 1920s. Its desk, reading stand, and food-and-drink compartments made it possible for the non-runner to spend weeks on end without taking a step. Many people were buried in it. (Some historians feel that the chair marked the beginning of Britain's decline as a world power.)

SOCKS

Some non-runners wear socks, while others just carry them. We feel that if worn, they should be worn on the feet. Wearing them loosely tied around your neck is considered gauche, except in Palm Springs, where it is the essence of chic. Some non-runners think a pair of socks adds needless weight, so they only wear one. Others insist on argyles. Whatever style you prefer, if your socks get wet or otherwise unpleasant, change them. Avoid sock hops, which cause excessive wear, and also avoid walking on nails or tacks, which could puncture your socks, damaging the fibers. If you feel insecure, wear support hosiery.

PANTS

Pants are popular with almost all non-runners, both male and female. Some prefer short pants, while others take the long chance. It was Abraham Lincoln who said that a man's pants should be long enough to cover his legs. The hairier the legs are, the truer this is. Thirty percent of lost body heat escapes through the kneecap, so what you cover them with is important. The rest of the heat escapes through heavy panting. Most non-runners will tell you to try to keep your pants on, if at all possible. In the winter, this is even more crucial, for fallen pants can quickly lead to frostbite of the nether extremities.

UNDERWEAR

Male non-runners like to argue over whether boxer shorts are preferable to briefs, whereas women generally are bored by this question. Should a non-runner wear a bra? Only if she is a woman, we think. Otherwise incarceration may result—or worse, an off-off-Broadway career. We think black satin lingerie is effective, too, especially for mixed-doubles non-running held in bedrooms.

Early attempts at non-running often failed because of technical problems. Here Marcia Kolonik, pioneer non-runner of the 1890s, attempts extended nap in the old Reverse L position, then believed to be effective.

Long johns can come in handy for winter non-running, unless you live in Fort Lauderdale.

HATS

Non-running is the best time to wear a hat, because it is then least likely to fall off. Some non-runners prefer a homburg because of its distinguished appearance. Others go for propeller beanies for an air of rakish insouciance. Politicians like hats for tossing when they tire of non-running. Calvin Coolidge, one of the greatest non-running presidents, enjoyed wearing Indian headdresses. These were considered old hat until Jimmy Carter revived the tradition. However, few considered wearing one a feather in his cap.

SHADES

Sunglasses are important, both to keep the sun out of your eyes and to keep people from seeing what color your eyes are. This can give them an unwelcome advantage. For non-running movie stars, dark glasses are, of course, de rigueur.

FALSE NOSES

Occasionally, we see a non-runner go by wearing one of those funny false-nose-eyeglass-mustache things. Frankly, we don't know why they do it, but if it helps them non-run, we say "fine." Perhaps it operates on the placebo principle. Non-runners often try to cover up their noses, particularly in the Orient, where noses are regarded as an embarrassment. We've always felt our noses are as much a part of us as our feet, except in cases where they've been replaced by plastic surgery. A non-runner with a nose job has always seemed to us a little out of his element. He'd probably be more comfortable ice fishing. (If a nose job doesn't "take," by the way, a temporary plastic nose can be purchased at any hardware store.)

HANKIES

As Dr. George Shoeshine, the non-runners' guru and dentist to the stars, often pointed out, "A non-runner should always carry a hankie, no matter where he is."

CREDIT CARDS

Most non-runners carry credit cards today, for the simple reason that they can be used to buy things. A good credit card should be made out of plastic and should have your name embossed on it, along with a lot of numbers. Many different styles and colors are available, some with racing stripes. Cards should be stored in your wallet. Wipe down once a week with a damp cloth.

CHAIRS

"What the hell do I need a chair for? I can sit on the floor." We heard this angry rebuke recently from one of the younger breed of non-runners, a lad of nineteen. It's true: You can sit on the floor—if that's your thing. But why eliminate so much variety from life? Chairs present an interesting challenge to the non-runner. They come in so many different styles and materials, from flimsy folding models to imperial thrones. We say get to know some chairs, try them out, talk to people who already own one. Every year, *Sitter's World*, the magazine of sitting, publishes its popular annual sitting issue, which compares models and selects a Chair of the Year. That's as good a place as any to start your quest.

COUCHES

A word about napping. Napping is one of the basic non-running activities. All you really need for it is a pair of eyes to close and a surface to plop your body onto. The best instrument for this purpose is a short, squat piece of equipment known as the couch.

Couches were made for naps. A couch is soft, but does not imply a lengthy commitment, as does a bed. A bed may be employed, however, in a pinch (although you must be careful whom you are pinching). In fact, you can use almost any surface that will accommodate the body in its horizontal state—a bathtub, a large rock, a throw rug, a kitchen counter, a park bench, or another person, provided it is one you know quite well.

STOPWATCHES

Stopwatches are totally unnecessary. All stopwatches will be confiscated at the border.

4

Staying Out of Shape

Too often we hear non-runners complaining because they are losing weight or feeling an urge to go out and play squash or challenge someone to a toboggan race. We warn them that they are in danger of becoming physical and should adopt a rigorous program of staying-out-of-shape exercises.

We have already covered the basic warming-down exercises for beginners in chapter 1. (Or was it chapter 2? Oh well, no matter.) The intermediate, advanced, or postgraduate non-runner needs more. He needs more complicated and interesting exercises to keep his mind off depression and suicide.

THE TRICKY THREE

These three exercises have been specially developed for the typical non-runner—sedentary, tired, passive, content to hang around and watch the store. Such a person may be low on strength and flexibility and needs to build up compensating abilities. We recommend the following:

1. TORSO HUG   Stand or sit. Grasp the torso of the nearest attractive person with both hands and arms. Hug firmly, while expressing endearments. Coo softly. Beg for some sign of affection. Alternate and repeat.
2. TAXI CALL   Raise the right hand as high in the air as possible while standing on tiptoe. With the left hand, cup the mouth and in a loud, shrill voice, shout: "Hey, taxi!" Repeat until it stops raining.
3. TV FLICK   Stand with the feet slightly apart. Bend at the knees. With the thumb and forefinger of the right hand, pull out the on-off knob. Wait for the picture. Flick the channel selector with the left hand. Jump two channels at a time. Allow your face to express irritation, even disgust. Try each channel twice. Sit back and read a magazine.

WAIT TRAINING

Wait training is invaluable to the non-runner. A supplemental wait-training program will increase your patience, as well as your stamina. You can find detailed programs and theories of wait training in a number of books (*Pumping Irony* by Addled Shortsnicker is a good one), but there are a few simple rules we'd like to mention.

The basic law of wait training is this: Never do today what you can put off until tomorrow. To build up your wait capacity you should have a long wait four or five times a week. Make a lot of doctor appointments, and schedule plenty of plane and train trips. You don't actually have to take the trips; it's enough just to pack a suitcase and go to the airport or train station and wait.

Movie lines are also excellent for wait training. Choose the hottest and trendiest movie in town, and pick a showing around eight p.m. on a Friday or Saturday night. Remember to continue breathing as you wait and don't grind your teeth or bite nails, neither yours or those of others. Improper waiting can result in injury, so don't overwait. If you find yourself growing tired, call it a night. (The relationship between non-running and movies is further explored in the chapter, "The Nine Greatest Non-Running Movies.")

YOGURT

Many non-runners have taken up yogurt for health and relaxation. Yogurt originally came from the far yeast. Now it comes from the supermarket. Walking there slowly while engaging in sex fantasies gets you started on the right path. After the yogurt is paid for, it must be carried home. Then a spoon must be found. (By this time, many non-runners are tired enough to take a nap. Others jump right into their yogurt.)

The spooning is all-important. Grasp the spoon in the first two fingers and thumb of either hand. Let the wrist do all the work. Spoon smoothly and accurately; don't try for too much speed. Remove the yogurt from the spoon with your mouth. Roll the yogurt around on your tongue. Count to six and swallow. Repeat until 160 calories are down. Rest.

GROAN EXERCISES

Nothing is as refreshing as a good groan, or as Jewish non-runners call it, a kvetch. Never be embarrassed or self-conscious about groaning. You've been through plenty and you have a right to complain. Sit down, legs outstretched. Recite every indignity heaped on you during the day; every instance in which you were cheated, bored, put upon, bullied, or baited. Name names. Leave nothing out. Scream if you wish. Pound the walls. Write your Congressman.

BRAIN-BUILDING

Recent research suggests that the brain is a large muscle whose mental capacity can be enlarged through proper exercise. For instance, Dr. Enzio Borzoi, chairman of the Mechanical Philosophy Department at Tufts University, started life as a retarded child but was able to increase his IQ to 197 after sending away for brain-building equipment in response to an ad he saw in *Tales from the Crypt Comics*. Here are several of the more effective brain exercises:

1. LOGICAL SPRINT   Stand with the cerebrum slightly bent, the frontal lobes crossed. Make ten complex statements that are strictly logical, yet contradict the conventional wisdom. Do not strain the cortex. Repeat, then say them backwards.
2. ABSTRACT REASONING STRETCH   Close your eyes and with all your might, try not to think of Alfred North Whitehead. Slowly bend forward from the cerebellum until you grow subjective. Think about the meaning of infinity. Think about the point where the universe ends and imagine what lies beyond it. Try not to black out.
3. EXTENDED MEMORY ROLL   Wrap your legs around your medulla oblongata. Begin reciting, in chronological order, the names of every person you have ever met in your life. When you're through, pour a stiff drink.

5

The Nonest Runner of Them All

The longest non-run of modern times is credited to Private Akiddel Eedivytoo, a Japanese soldier who spent twenty-nine years on an island in the South Pacific. His story is one of dedication, oversight, sunburn, years of humming, near-tragedy, and discovery.

Akiddel was ordered to guard the entrance to a cave that had a terrific view of the harbor. He stayed at his post for seven hours under a broiling sun. Not surprisingly, he fell asleep. Had he been awake he would have seen his fellow soldiers leave the island. The date was one he would never forget—June 12, 1943. (Actually, he forgot it for a few weeks in August of 1956 but it came back to him during a nosebleed in September.)

For the twenty-nine years that he remained at his post, Akiddel nibbled on a candy bar. To pass the time he would write songs. Before he ran out of room on the candy wrapper, he composed "Inka Dinka Doo," "Can't Help Lovin' Dat Man of Mine" and the first act of an opera he called "Steelers 21, Dolphins 17."

He was discovered when a bottle of Tabasco sauce into which he'd stuffed the candy wrapper was picked up by an Australian fishing boat. Jock Hughes, skipper of the *Lyndon B.*, opened the bottle and began reading what he thought was a note. "Inka dinka doo, adink a doo, adink a dee . . . "

"Sounds like Japanese," his son said.

Akiddel was found the next morning. Jock Hughes tells the touching story in his best-selling book, *I'm OK, You Need a Shave.*

"When we finally convinced him that the war was over and we were his friends (or would be as soon as he had a shower) he told us of his great shame.

"After not running for the first twenty-three years on the island, he weakened. He ran to the other side of the island hoping to find a piano. While running, he tripped, fell down, and cut his knee. His uniform had a grass stain on it and he made us promise we would take him to a dry cleaner before his commanding officer saw him. He cursed himself for being a weakling, convinced that running would cost him a corporal's stripe."

EPILOGUE   Akiddel Eedivytoo today sits home and collects royalties on a popular Japanese paperweight that bears his likeness. He is a millionaire, though still a private (ret.).

Clement Croyable of Paris (707) takes slight lead against wedge of Brie (95) in finals of 1968 All-European Human vs. Cheese Non-Running Championships. Brie later pulled ahead when Croyable's nose began to run, but it could not sustain the grueling pace and began dramatically running all over the table, allowing Croyable to overtake it and clinch victory. Croyable retired from non-running competition the following year after losing match race to an unseeded Tilsit from Detroit.

6

Myth or Fallacy:
The Non-Runner's Quiz

Like any fast-growing popular phenomenon, non-running has dragged with it a similarly exploding body of information, much of it contradictory and confusing. Misunderstanding abounds. Many have difficulty sorting through the cascade of tips, rumors, legends, gossip, lies, and dirty jokes to ferret out the hard nuggets of truth. The purpose of this quiz is to help set your mind straight once and for all.

Some of the following statements are merely myths, while others are outright fallacies. Figure out which are which, then simply mark each statement *F* or *M* and hope for the best.

1. There are more non-runners alive today than there have ever been dead non-runners in all history.
2. The first sneaker was cut from an old inner tube in Missouri in 1912 by a former slave who was trying to invent basketball.
3. At the Yerkes Primate Laboratory, overweight chimpanzees have been taught to urinate contemptuously into Adidas running shoes.
4. Non-running is fattening.
5. Non-running is non-fattening.
6. Fat runs downhill.
7. Non-running causes permanent damage to couches.
8. Snakes have been seen non-running.
9. Oysters down in Oyster Bay do it.
10. Goldfish in the privacy of bowls do it.
11. Nine out of ten non-runners will, under no circumstances, have anything to do with a quiz, test, or examination of any kind.

Science and technology continue to foster progress in physical development. Here Edmund and Norbert Zagotz (standing), brothers who developed the Zagotz Trainer, a breakthrough in mechanical body-toughening aids, demonstrate their invention for Fred Edema, a vice president of General Techtronics. Edema later announced that he was enormously impressed and would recommend that GT go into immediate production of the fitness-building machine as soon as he stopped leaking.

12. People who maintain physical fatness remain dead longer than early risers.
13. In the sixteenth century, exercising was considered sinful.
14. In the twentieth century, sin is considered a good form of exercise.
15. Superman never worked out, but was stronger than anyone.
16. Joggers never smile.
17. Even when you're sweating from head to toe, your feet will feel dry in Sportwick Socks.
18. President Carter has proclaimed December 17–23 National Non-Running Week and ordered all federal employes to sit down for those seven days.
19. Ralph Nader said non-running is safe at any speed.
20. Peanut butter smeared on your feet will prevent blisters.
21. Australia is the only country where non-running is a felony.
22. Buzz Aldrin was the first man to non-run on the moon.
23. Izzy Baldwin was the first man to moon while non-running.
24. Macaroons are a staple in the Cameroons.
25. Vidal Sassoon is often festooned in maroon.
26. Non-running has a tendency to make writers rampantly silly.

ANSWERS: Answers to questions in this quiz may be found in our soon-to-be-published next book, *The Psychosexual Implications of Non-Running*.

7 🐢

The Non-Runner's Diet

Several of our friends were beginning a marathon non-run when Phil (the Plate) Starchberg came by. Phil had been non-running since high-school, where his classmates voted him Least Likely to Move a Muscle.

We were genuinely surprised to see Phil because he so rarely leaves home. Years ago Phil lived in a three-room apartment. He left, he explained, because the temptation was too great to stand up and stroll from one room to another.

He moved into a single room: a kitchen. Not surprisingly, Phil became the Father of the Non-Runner's Diet. Here's Phil's diet.

MONDAY

Eat all you want. Try not to stop. Roll your sleeves past your elbows and dig in with both hands. Grunting is permissible. On days like this, you may even think about eating wood. Go ahead. Nobody ever gets painful stomach splints. WARNING: The slipcovers on your couch may be the same color as certain foods. Red slipcovers, for example, have been mistaken for a full meal of tomato juice, rare roast beef, radishes, strawberry yogurt and a modest beaujolais. Don't make the mistake of eating your couch.

TUESDAY

Relax. Most of this day will be spent mopping up the food you spilled Monday. Call the grocery store and identify yourself. Ask them to deliver a lot of stuff. Chuckle along with them when they say, "Sounds like old man Finkle is having a rough Tuesday." (Substitute your name. It may not be Finkle. You may even be a woman not named Finkle.)

WEDNESDAY

Another slow day. It's probably a good idea to chew your food. Use silverware.

THURSDAY

You may need cheering up. Call a runner. Say the words *chocolate pudding, cashew nuts, jelly doughnut, lemon meringue pie.* Hang up and pat yourself on the back. This should exhaust you. Sleep will follow. Dream about food.

FRIDAY

BREAKFAST   Glass of fresh or frozen orange juice (4 oz.)
One buckwheat pancake
One rounded tsp. sugar
Coffee, no cream

LUNCH   Chicken rice soup, one serving
Carrot and raisin salad, 4 heaping tbsps.
Iced tea

DINNER   Fried fish, one fillet
Beets, 2/3 cup
Skim milk, 8 oz.
Applesauce, 4 oz., unsweetened.

SATURDAY

Thank God it's not Friday. Eat. Drink. Be merry. Whooppeeeee!

SUNDAY

A new running and exercise book will appear on the bestseller list. This certainty will take the fun out of eating. The food in your mouth tastes like sneakers. The crumbs on your couch aren't as much fun. You're out of Scotch and the liquor stores are closed.

The shouts of Sunday runners will come through your open window. There's nothing you can do about it. Don't bother closing your window. Then you won't quite hear what they're saying and you'll think you're missing something. You're a non-runner. And you'll feel better on Monday.

DIET RULES FOR NON-RUNNERS

1. Keep a flashlight near your refrigerator.
2. Frozen foods go in the top part of your refrigerator. (Some non-runners prefer the designation "freezer.")
3. When the refrigerator door opens, a little light goes on. This light is not thought to be on when the door is closed. But who really knows?
4. If the refrigerator door opens and the little light doesn't come on, buy a new bulb.
5. Install the new bulb in a hurry. If you take too much time the refrigerator will accumulate too much hot air, causing severe schizophrenia.
6. Open the door. If the light still doesn't come on, you know it isn't the bulb's fault.
7. Open the door again. What have you got to lose? Maybe the light'll come on this time.
8. If the light still hasn't come on, you are the owner of two perfectly good refrigerator light bulbs.
9. Good thing we told you about Rule No. 1.

THOUGHT FOR FOOD

"You've got your food. What do you do now?" we asked John, who works behind the counter at our favorite luncheonette.

"Eat it," John told us.

PROPER SIZE AND WEIGHT

Non-runners come in all sizes and shapes. Just like buildings. Since buildings rarely go anywhere and are often found in the same place day after day, a lot of people tend to confuse buildings and non-runners. Figs. 1 and 2 should help.

Fig. 1   *Building*   Fig. 2   *Non-runner*

FOODS TO AVOID

The National Federation of Non-Runners says everything is okay except food your mother says is good for you. The federation spends millions of dollars a year testing stuff that food manufacturers send them. The federation staff also cuts costs by stealing a lot of the food they test. How can your mom match that kind of operation? This is not meant to detract from Mom's knowledge in other areas. For instance, tests have proven that it's just as easy to love a rich person as a poor person.

CARBO-UNLOADING

The runner believes that pushing down a lot of carbohydrates before a race is a great idea. He calls that carbo-loading. As a result, supermarkets are usually completely out of spaghetti, macaroni, white bread, and other carbo products for weeks before a big race. Since these yo-yos run big races at the drop of a T-shirt, the non-runner is frequently the unintentional victim of Carbo-Unloading. The National Federation does have a list of stores that stock carbos for non-runners. Unfortunately, gangs of runners have begun looting these stores. In those areas where looting is unusually high, the federation has established carbo speakeasies. These can usually be found beneath white-clam-sauce speakeasies.

We enjoyed a plate of spaghetti recently at a carbo speak-easy that was disguised as a dry-cleaning establishment. Since runners are always on the lookout for these illegal carbo parlors, we were forced to eat the spaghetti out of the pockets of a brown tweed jacket.

MIDNIGHT SNACKS

You have non-run for several hours and are ready for bed. But you want a little something to breathe on Mr. Sandman. What should that be? Our method of deciding is simple. We close our eyes, open the refrigerator, and reach inside. We eat whatever we pull out. Beer, eggs, baking soda, anything. Well, not *any*thing. We never keep bananas in the refrigerator, no-no-no-no.

8

The Zen of Sitting

Veteran sitters find that strange things begin happening to them once they sit down.

Their anxiety diminishes. They become less irritable and tired. Their stress and tension are reduced. They are suddenly able to relax all the major muscle groups in the lower half of their bodies, something that was impossible only seconds before. And, most important, their laps return.

We have spoken to many sitters and virtually all of them

report these subtle changes that come over them during the sitting process.

"It's like these subtle changes come over me during the sitting process," says Nan Gowonow, an attractive young baby-sitter from East Quogue, Long Island. "Sitting gives me a sense of controlling my own life. I like the finiteness of a good sit, the fact that it has a clear beginning and end. I like the feel of my butt striking the chair squarely and the strong sense of place that comes from being well-seated. It makes me feel firmly rooted and in touch with the planet."

Tolbert Feldspar is in his early thirties. For years he was bothered by dizziness. "All the time I was dizzy," he told us. "Dizzy, then nauseous." Then he started sittting down. Though it did not cure his dizziness, it made him less tired. "Sitting is my favorite part of the day," he said. "All morning I'm on my feet (he's a ticket-taker on a merry-go-round), and I look forward to lunchtime when I can sit down. It gives my life meaning. It's not just a means of relaxing, it's life itself. It defines me. I sit—therefore I am."

Generally considered the world's foremost sitter is Thor Baldescu, the Rumanian relaxing champion and holder of many sitting and leaning records. "It's all in the backbone," he told a recent seminar in sitting studies held in Bucharest, as he joyfully plopped on his unprotesting coccyx.

Sitting may be done anywhere, even on the ground (though this may dirty the pants). But Baldescu says that the serious sitter requires a chair. Chairs conform to the body structure of a sitting person. "To sit correctly, the body must 'fold' twice—at the knees and at the pelvis," Baldescu contends. "Otherwise, you are just lying around."

A properly fitted chair will provide support on two planes, horizontal and vertical. The horizontal is the more important of the two and must be adjusted at a precise distance from the ground so that the sitter's feet rest lightly on the floor. "Dangling feet are a sure sign that something's wrong," contends Baldescu. "Either you've got a poorly built chair or your legs need adjusting." Baldescu himself carries a custom-made

The body of veteran miler Eleanora Crantz was found in this locker room after a recent race in Springfield, Illinois. Autopsy showed that Ms. Crantz's blood had rushed to her feet during race (a common occurrence), causing oxygen-starved brain to malfunction. Unable to remember her locker combination, the desperate Crantz attempted to batter locker open with her skull.

plastic folding chair everywhere so he can practice no matter where he is.

He is a firm believer in the mental side of sitting and, to experience it more fully, will often sit on his head. This causes blood to rush to the head, increasing the brain's sensitivity.

But the real joy of sitting, according to Baldescu, comes in the second hour of being seated, when the body attains a higher emotional state. "The head begins to drop back and the mouth falls open," he says. "The eyelids close. You feel incredible inner peace." Still later, yet a new level is reached in which the sitter experiences surreal fantasy states filled with symbolic visual imagery.

Eastern mystics have long recognized this phenomenon, which marathon sitters, who have their own colorful jargon, call "catching your Zs." Zen Buddhists refer to it as horizontal transcendentistry, a state in which one often loses his sense of identity and feels at one with his teeth and gums. The Tibetan lama Dhuru Bun-Zetz frequently counseled his disciples: "To sit is to know. To know is to sit. When I am well sat, I am not merely one man sitting; *I am sitting itself*. I am at one with all other sitters of the universe. Do you follow me? If not, sit down; then you'll know."

These euphoric feelings described by sitters and seated gurus have been scientifically documented. Researchers have found that sitting relaxes a tense body and that men and women who sit down regularly release greater levels of the hormone sedenephrine into their blood. This hormone, according to Dr. Fritz Langerhaltz, a distinguished Westphalian biochemist, is "the chemical basis for joke manufacturing in the body." Thus, sitting increases the brain's capacity to invent funny jokes and riddles, leading to a good-humored, relaxed, easy-going state. This goes a long way toward explaining the often-noted fact that jokes are never made by people who are running.

Sitting also has psychological reverberations. "The buttocks are the seat of the emotions," says Dr. Fern Gottwort, a well-known behavioral proctologist from San Francisco. "Hence the phrase, 'I'm sitting on top of the world.' " Dr. Gottwort has em-

Park bench habitually used by Bernard N. Garbanzo of Duluth, the first man in Minnesota to sit down. At first regarded as a Communist agitator, Garbanzo spread his doctrine that sitting promoted good circulation until, in 1901, sitting down became standard practice in all midwestern schools.

ployed sitting extensively in her therapy and reports that numerous patients have shown improvement after being treated. She was able to calm a seriously nervous housewife in Kennebunkport, Maine, who had called for help on a high-anxiety hotline, by advising her to stop trying to get the house germfree in time for her mother-in-law's visit and instead sit down for fifteen minutes and rest. The woman was later able to successfully raise a family of four and learn gourmet Chinese cooking.

To produce the desired altered state of unconsciousness in some of her more highly disturbed patients, the ones she has clinically diagnosed as "nervous wrecks," or "whackos," Dr. Gottwort will often strap them to chairs and strike them in the cranial area with wooden mallets. This helps induce "penetration into the other world," as it is known to researchers.

Dr. Gottwort says that any sitter can reach this state on his own simply by sitting in a comfortable chair, relaxing, taking three deep breaths, and rapping his head sharply against a wall six or seven times. The onset of altered unconsciousness is usually signaled by the well-known "seeing stars" effect. This quickly passes and is replaced by a dark, quiet phase.

We are only beginning to understand the relationship between sitting and the mind. Ironically, in this area the so-called primitive people of the world may be far ahead of the societies we like to think of as more advanced. The Tularemia Indians of southern Iran, for instance, live in the mountains, where they sit together in large groups of over a hundred people for days on end without any sign of movement at all. In the middle of eland hunts, the aborigine Bushmen of the Swedish Kalahari often sit down for no apparent reason and lose their quarry, saying only that they are "tired." These people apparently know instinctively or through tribal tradition the benefits that come from sitting. It is interesting to note that among both these peoples, paranoid schizophrenia, which has reached epidemic proportions in the industrial West, is virtually unknown.

9 🐢

A Nap with a Champion

We are in the living room of Walt Torpo of Claverack, New York, an Olympic-level non-runner and one of the world's slowest humans. He is asleep. His style is wondrously natural. He sleeps without a sound, leaning back comfortably in an old brown leather Barcalounger, his head tipped slightly rearward, his balance perfect, his posture loose but not slouched. In the past month, he has slept each day more than he has stayed awake. He has missed fourteen meals and innumerable newspapers. He is hungry and needs to go to the bathroom.

But moving seems like more trouble than it's worth, he has told us. Occasionally, his eyes pop open with an audible click and he cracks a joke, then reverts instantly to sleep. He is wearing an orange silk bathrobe over his plump body. It is late evening and the house is overheated, the way he likes it. The TV is on loud and the dog is barking. None of this bothers him. He has incredible concentration. He once napped straight through the Battle of the Bulge, remaining unawakened even when a German tank ran over his foxhole.

Torpo is in his middle fifties, just the age when nappers come into their prime, but he looks like a child of twelve. He is five feet two and a half inches tall and weighs 197 pounds. His hair is fluffy blond, his eyelids ever so delicately veined. As he naps, his body works smoothly and efficiently, every part operating in harmony with every other. His stomach gently rises and falls, as though regulated by the rhythm of his breathing. His pulse beats quietly and without fuss. He never snores, no matter how long his nap goes on.

"Snoring wastes energy," he says, his eyelids suddenly clicking open in that alarming way they do. "I used to snore as a

46

kid. Tried everything to quit. Finally, I went to Albany to an ear-nose-throat man. He made me put my head back, poured LePage's Mucilage into each nostril, told me to let it harden, keep it in there for two weeks. Then I went back and he removed it. After that, I never snored again."

We are here napping with Torpo because we hope to find out how a world-class non-runner looks at his craft and what he thinks about after he is asleep. We ask him how he first became a non-runner. There is no answer, for once again he has drifted off. We discuss the possibility of waking him but decide it would be impolite. Eventually, we fall asleep too, despite the excitement of being in his presence. Hours later, we are awakened by Torpo's droning voice.

"I was great at sports," he is saying, "but my eyes were bad so I kept running into things. Loved baseball. At bat I had plenty of power, but I always struck out. In the field, I had a great arm but I could never find the ball in time to throw anyone out. Once I tried to steal second and ran into the dugout. I got called names a lot. But even in grade school, I had this talent. I was slower than anyone. I always loved to sit down. I could loiter better than any other kid. In the mornings, my mother could never get me out of bed. I guess I felt safe there because I couldn't run into anything."

He looks at his watch. "Ah," he says. "Time for my favorite." With surpassing economy of motion, his hand moves gracefully toward the table next to him, where it deftly grasps a small metal object. "Love Donny and Marie," he says, flicking a switch. The channel on the TV set changes instantly.

"Care for a beer?" he asks. We accept.

"Rosalie," he calls. Immediately, his wife appears, bearing three frosty mugs of beer. Rosalie has curly red hair and a mocking half-smile. She is quite a non-runner herself. She and Torpo met in 1958 in a car crash on the New York State Thruway. Recovering in the hospital, they discovered they both had a broken left leg.

It was Rosalie who encouraged Walt to retire at age forty and take it easy. "Don't worry about the money," she told him.

"God will provide." He had been working as a stop-sign in Wappingers Falls and spending his off-duty hours leaning against the counter in a bait-and-tackle shop run by his friend, Charlie Wigand, watching people buy fishing gear.

"One day, Charlie suggested that I lie down in the back," says Torpo. "He had this old couch back there. So I tried it. It had been so long since I'd taken a nap, I couldn't even remember what it was like. When I woke up I felt fantastic and I remember saying to myself: *This is fantastic. I've got to do this some more.* So I started napping at home too. At first, I could only go for short times. Maybe twenty-five minutes, tops. I thought, *I will never break 45:15.* I was so sure it would never happen." He laughs.

As Torpo speaks, Donny and Marie are roller-skating around a sneering Paul Lynde, while singing a poignant ballad. Torpo has not missed a beat, even while talking. A solitary forefinger taps rhythmically on the chair arm. The eyes close again. Over the years, Torpo has developed the uncanny knack of aligning his nap patterns to the TV programming. He catnaps during commercials and dull spots. Somehow, as soon as the commercial ends, Torpo's eyes open. Snap! He himself is incapable of explaining this ability. "They say the commercials are broadcast louder than the regular programs," he says. "Maybe that's it. Maybe I'm sensitive to the volume. I don't know. I just do it."

Torpo has already finished his beer and calls for another. It's all we can do to catch up. Our glasses are still half full and we've been gulping. He begins talking about his future, as Rosalie arrives with a fresh mug. She trips and it spills all over him. Torpo doesn't seem to notice.

"I'd like to get myself ready for a really serious effort," he says. "I'm going to attempt to nap standing up. Freestyle—no leaning. I think that might get me on 'The Gong Show.' Then I could settle back for a nice long snooze."

We look around the room. It is filled with the evidence of Torpo's accomplishment. It's a pleasant, dark room with heavy shades fully drawn. There are many easy chairs and couches and thick rugs. Torpo sits in the flickering TV light, seemingly in a reverie halfway between sleep and consciousness. Rosalie stands just behind him, savagely mimicking his every move. It occurs to us that we are sitting a foot or so from one of the most perfect non-running machines on earth. If you asked a brilliant physicist to invent an efficient, high-powered engine designed expressly to idle, chances are he would come up with Walt Torpo.

We ask Walt whether he has any advice for beginners. "Sure," he says. But the rest of the advice never comes. Walt's eyes are closed again. We look at each other and shrug. Then we quietly rise, wave good-bye to Rosalie, and walk into the warm night air.

10 🐢

Non-Running in the People's Republic

On our trip to China in the fall of 1977, we were surprised and pleased to see that non-running had made great strides in the People's Republic. Wherever we went, the Chinese people were out not running in great numbers. Often, eight or nine hundred thousand people were doing it in unison, always with great enthusiasm and unfailing politeness.

Our guide and interpreter, a demure young lady named Nyot Yet, explained that in China all non-running is conducted according to Marxist-Leninist principles which emphasize class struggle and intense work to defeat delusionary bourgeois thinking.

She told us that Chairman Mao himself had taken the lead in People's non-running, often exhorting other party officials to follow his example. He wrote of his non-running experience in a popular 1954 poem titled, "Dare to Strive Toward Perfection in Non-Running Through the Resolution of Internal Contradictions Among Party Cadres, and Would Somebody Please Get Me a Cup of Tea." In 1967, Chairman Mao led the entire nation in a heroic leaning against the Great Wall to demonstrate that even while resting one could still struggle against imperialism.

After the Chairman's death, Nyot Yet told us, there had been a short period of improper veering from correct principles, during which the notorious Gang of Four had sown confusion by advocating hopping on one foot with both eyes closed. This caused many people to fall from the path of true socialism and sustain serious injuries. As it turned out, of course, the Gang members were revealed to be running dogs of capitalism, and overthrown. With their downfall, non-running was placed back on its proper footing and everyone felt much relaxed.

Wherever we went in China, whether to farms, small towns, or big bustling cities, we met people sincerely interested in showing us their non-running techniques and in learning about ours. We remember Dang Wok, an old hot-pepper camouflager on a diced-chicken-with-walnuts farm in Szechwan Province who told us how difficult non-running had been back in the days before the revolution, with its collectivization of all non-running activities. Then there was Sey Wen, a mother of sixteen from Tientsin, who related how she had been unenthusiastic about non-running until a session with her local District Committee to Correct Backward Thinking and Straighten Out Counter-Revolutionarily Inclined Soreheads brought her to an understanding of its many benefits.

These were just two of the approximately sixteen million people who indicated to us in casual conversation how exciting a part non-running plays in their everyday lives.

Of course, the People's Republic is a big place and in our three-days, five-nights excursion, it was possible to see only the highlights. On our return, some people suggested that perhaps we saw only what the authorities wanted us to see. To some extent that may be true. Even so, the cheerfulness and sheer enthusiasm of the non-runners we met left us with the feeling that the potential for cooperation between non-runners of all races and nations is greater now than at any other time in history.

11

Sam Speed, Private Foot

The only thing moving in my office was the bubble in the water cooler. I stared out the window and wondered if the clock in the Forsythe Tower had been replaced by a $1.98 carillon. No, the Forsythe had been blown up three years ago to make room for an unpainted-furniture store. That ringing was my phone. I told it to stop but it wasn't in a listening mood. Well, friend, two can play that game.

"For one point," I hollered, "where are boxing matches held?"

R-r-r-ring.

"Precisely. For another point, can you tell me the first name of a short-story writer whose last name was Lardner?"

R-r-r-ring.

"Splendid. And where do politicians toss their hat?"

R-r-r-ring.

"Good. In geometry, what do we call the area or space between two concentric circles? This is for all the marbles."

There was no sound.

"You were on the right track just a few seconds ago."

Nothing.

"This could mean an F."

I was interrupted by a knock on my office door. A tall blonde walked into the room. She was dressed all in brown tweed,

Coach Will Twombley shouts encouragement to Fred Farkas (center), famed non-runner of the forties, who regularly challenged and defeated veteran runners. He is seen here charging for the lead in the 1943 Dust Bowl Supermarathon. Runners were at a loss to explain how Farkas continually beat them to finish lines, in view of the fact that his feet never left the ground.

except for a wool scarf that was so bulky it seemed to be hiding something.

"What's that around your collar?" I asked.

"Ring," she said, flashing a smile that let me know she'd been in the doorway too long.

"Do you mind if I sit down? I may have a case for you. I was told you were good at confidential matters."

"I've got a lousy memory, if that's what you mean."

"It's my grandmother. We're all very worried about her. We're—" She started to sob into a handkerchief that wasn't nearly as big as a parachute.

There was nothing I could do. So I counted the pencils standing on my desk in a wedge of Parmesan cheese. She cried. I checked the back of my hands for liver spots. I used a rubber band to shoot a paper clip out the window. I hoped we weren't on "Candid Camera."

She began to fold the handkerchief and I suggested a Marine color guard. "I'm sorry. It's just that this is so hard to tell a stranger. My grandmother—"

I ripped the handkerchief out of her hands and wrung it out over my poinsettia. "Let me try and see if I can figure it out. Your grandmother's started running, right?"

"My God, yes. That's it exactly. How did you know?"

I used the same modest shrug that made millions for Jimmy Stewart. "I'm getting a lot of cases like that these days. If it's any consolation, you're not alone. A lot of people are running without any thought of what it does to the family. Years of respect built up in one neighborhood, a wonderful relationship with the girl at the express check-out counter, and then one day your grandmother races by the firehouse in purple shorts—"

"Red shorts. Past the pool hall."

"Yes, I've been called in on several of these cases. Did the Webster family send you here? the Goldbergs? the Johnsons?"

"The Johnsons. You stopped their great-aunt Ethel."

"Yeah, Ethel Johnson. Nice old girl. Choppy stride. Kept her hands too high. How's she doing lately?"

"Sits on a couch all day long eating Sugar Frosted Flakes

and carving the faces of presidents on avocado pits. The family couldn't be happier."

"Great. I just heard from the Goldbergs myself. I stopped their grandmother Bertha from running. Wide feet, too much of a push in her stride. She's great now. Hasn't left her bedroom in four months."

"Do you think you can do for my grandmother what you did for the Johnsons' Aunt Ethel?"

"Hard to say. It'll take a pile of avocado pits."

"We can afford it. We're wealthy. Here."

She undid the knot in her handkerchief and a checkbook fell out. "Make it for two thousand," I told her. She scribbled the check and tore it out of her book.

"Fine. I'll let you know when I get some results. Shouldn't take long."

"But don't you have to know my grandmother's name, where she runs, when she runs, her time for the half-mile?"

I took all the information and tried not to look bored. That was careless, not asking any of those questions on my own. The only thing that can sink my little game is carelessness.

She left. I was out the door a few minutes later, heading for the small park her grandmother ran around each day. We met at the usual place, the frankfurter wagon.

"How much did you get?" the old girl asked.

"Five hundred," I said. It's easy to lie to old people. "But you've really got the family worried. If you ran for another month I could probably get them up to five thousand."

"Another month and I'll kill myself. You and I will split the money just like you split it with Bertha Goldberg and Ethel Johnson and all the rest. We didn't get into it for the money. You know that."

She was right. The money was my reward. The old girls thought up the scheme and they needed somebody to play along. That was me. Sam Speed, Private Foot.

I wanted to get back to my office but I knew what was coming. This was the part they couldn't get enough of.

"So tell me," the old girl said. "My rotten granddaughter

came alone or she was with her no-good husband, the college professor who can't let an old lady watch Baretta?"

"Alone."

"Sure. You know the only time he talks to me is when I take too long in the bathroom. And he gets up so early it's hard for me to beat him to the toilet."

I nodded.

"My granddaughter—was she crying?"

"Buckets. She brought along Wilt Chamberlain's T-shirt."

"Ha. I bought her that handkerchief. But do you think she remembers? Let me tell you something. . . ."

She was still going strong when an old party in a green and yellow sweat suit trotted by. He must have been eighty.

"That's Mr. Bethany," the old girl said. "What a rotten family he's got. You'll be hearing from the daughter soon."

I nodded. She kept talking. Mr. Bethany was moving too quickly. I'd have to warn him about that. No use killing a good thing.

12

How to Find the Time

Hyman Ganoosh (not his real name) is a three-time Olympic marathon champion who has an exclusive endorsement contract with a famous breakfast cereal and his own line of designer running shorts. He races hard and he trains hard. For years he has spent four or five hours a day running through the streets of downtown Cleveland (not its real name). Clevelanders are used to seeing his lithe form speeding through the avenues and byways of their city. Kids wave and traffic cops salute him as he zooms by. Cars screech to a friendly halt, often barely missing him.

But in truth, Hyman Ganoosh is no longer what he seems. Three years ago, he came to an important decision: He was sick of running. Couldn't stand it. His legs ached like crazy. His toes tingled with pain. His training routine bored him silly. Ganoosh (still not his real name) had made a pile of dough off his TV commercials and the book written under his name, and he figured he didn't need to torture himself anymore.

He started cutting down his daily runs. He would jog a few blocks, then duck into an alley, put on a raincoat he'd carried wadded up under his shirt, and catch a cab to another part of town, where he would jog a few more blocks. He'd repeat this several times until people all over town had spotted him running by. Soon even this routine became too grueling, and Ganoosh hired a double to do his running for him.

While the double ran, Ganoosh would duck into a neighborhood bar and order a Bloody Mary. There he would be joined by three old friends, a college cross-country star, a champion hurdler, and a podiatrist who writes best-selling paperbacks about runners' feet. All of them wore ski masks.

These people are typical closet non-runners, and their numbers are growing. They have a common problem faced by many non-runners: How to find the time and energy for not running?

We have a friend named Sir Sagramore, a tall, handsome truffle grower in his late twenties (not his real approximate age). He knows he exercises too much. He jogs once a day, plays tennis at lunch, and golf early in the morning; he skis in winter, swims in summer, and rakes in fall. He knows he should be spending more time at work and at home, but the pressures of a highly structured competitive sports program have kept him constantly on the go. "I've been a jock my whole life," he told us. "It's all I know." Still, he asked us if there was anything he could do. We suggested he set aside just fifteen minutes a day for staring out the window at nothing in particular. He burst into tears. "I just don't have the time," he said. "My schedule's figured to the second."

We explained to Sir Sagramore that time isn't hard to find if you know where it's kept. Many successful exercisers lie down regularly. The trick is to analyze your schedule and find the hidden time pockets when non-running can be squeezed in. (One thinks of the great football star Bronco Nagurski (his real name), who'd catch a quick snooze at the bottom of pileups.)

Some people have found that instead of jogging between home and work each day they can catch a bus or taxi, thus saving precious time that would have been spent running. For habitual lunchtime runners, it's often convenient to look for a restaurant along the route. There you are allowed to sit down and have a meal, which will take a load off your feet and build up your pep. (Many people realize that food is a kind of fuel that your body converts to energy almost as an engine burns gas, but too few understand that it also tastes good.)

The easiest time for non-running is the middle of the night. This is when you are least likely to be distracted by people looking for someone to play right field in a softball game. Set your alarm to wake you at around three or four a.m., steal quietly from your bed, and lie down for a nap on your living room couch.

Sometimes, circumstances make it difficult for even the most avid non-runner to non-run avidly. For instance, you might be in the middle of an important tennis game when the need to non-run comes over you. A friend of ours, Harley Bodeen (not his real first name, but his real last name) once found himself in that situation. In mid-serve he had to simulate a pulled muscle and limp to the sidelines, where he spent five minutes of satisfying non-movement, moaning loudly the whole time. After returning to the game, he felt so relaxed and his opponent was so disgusted with his antics, that he won easily. He later decided to change his name to Hyman Ganoosh, but that's another story.

13 🐢

Non-Running and the Senior Citizen

Non-Runners International asked Dr. Rex Gamble, famed for his experiments with dead hamsters, to test non-runners of all ages. Contributing to the latest issue of *Medical Nonsense*, Dr. Gamble wrote, "I thought of non-running as a fad, a craze, an activity for the not-now generation. I was prepared to have nothing to do with a group of Weird Wallies who advocated proper dress, proper diet, and proper exercise for a movement as suspect as non-running.

"I could imagine what my colleagues would say when I told them that old Rex was moving into non-running. Some real sharp Latin thing like 'Sic semper tyrannis, Rex.' No, sir, that wasn't about to happen to yours truly, a Golden Stethoscope winner six of the last seven years. Non-running, I figured, could take a hike. That was before a call from my broker. He told me that my holdings in United Licorice were worthless. My portfolio, he said, was lying face down on the floor of the stock exchange, and junior clerks were using my certificates as a Carioca practice area."

What follows from Dr. Gamble is a lot more humble. And very much on the side of non-running.

"I have taken the trouble," Dr. Gamble grumbles, "to divide older non-runners into three categories. I call the first of these Category A. The reason for this division of categories was to keep the older non-runners from hanging out together and flaunting their Social Security checks.

"I compared the life-styles of thousands of older non-runners and runners. (Or, as I call the second group, Gray Panters.)

Almost typical are two senior citizens to whom I shall refer as Nutsy and Oliver Wendell Holmes."

Nutsy, who runs, left his shabby apartment in baggy shorts and a T-shirt emblazoned with the legend, "Machine wash warm, tumble dry medium." Mr. Holmes emerged from his home in a dark blue blazer, gray slacks, and a white turtleneck. (He dresses himself.) Mr. Holmes turned a corner, counted forty steps, and pushed open the door of the Rub-a-Dub Pub. His gin and tonic was waiting for him. He drank four in just under an hour and left, his hair falling over his eyes, and narrowly avoided a collision with Nutsy, who was finishing his run, his hair falling over his eyes.

Safely home, Mr. Holmes napped. Nutsy proceeded to a neighborhood bookstore, where he shelled out $9.95 for *The Joy of Fatigue*. That evening, Nutsy fashioned himself a dinner omelette of curds and whey. Mr. Holmes counted the same thirty steps and pushed into the Rub-a-Dub. His martini was waiting for him. And so was Helga, runner-up for Miss Sweden of 1976 in the most competitive contest that country had ever known.

When Dr. Gamble said good night to his two subjects, Nutsy was ironing his T-shirt in front of the television screen, turning the channel selector in an effort to find O. J. Simpson running through the airport. Mr. Holmes was giving Helga an English lesson, pausing only to say a silent prayer to the god who provides for runners and non-runners, without regard to color, creed, or race (especially race), for making Helga such an eager and slow pupil.

"The older runner, if he is still alive, is a truly happy person," Dr. Gamble writes. "I was recently a visitor to the home of Dutch (Crazy Thumbs) Klenzer, the famous bootlegger and mass murderer of the twenties, thirties, and forties. Dutch told me that he'd thought the only way to avoid capture for all those years was by constantly being on the run. He now realizes that was a tragic mistake. The best thing he ever did was to stop running and start plea bargaining."

"Whenever I think of how stupid I was back then," Dutch confessed to Dr. Gamble, "I feel like hitting myself on the head with a month-old Kaiser roll. What a pain. Gives me gas just to think about it. Make a shooting someplace in New Hampshire and then I gotta run, like a nut, to a hideout in Vermont. Worst food I ever tasted. And the bathroom was a hollowed-out saxophone case. Plus which, the landlady knew all my jokes. Don't know how long I was there. Got so weak I couldn't turn the pages on the calendar. My rifle went on the blink, my radio was on the fritz, and my backhand was hopelessly inept."

Dr. Gamble recognized those symptoms as running's little-known side effects.

"Natch," Dutch said. "Anyway, one morning I wake up because the alarm clock someplace is going bing-bing-bing like a police bell and I figured I had to get outta there. No cops is gonna pull an Anne Frank on Dutch (Crazy Thumbs) Klenzer. So now I'm on the run again. You know how may states a man can shoot somebody in and how many states he can run to and hide? You got any idea at all? Take a guess. I give you a million guesses and you wouldn't come close. Here's a hint. I'm only talking states in continental America. Go ahead, guess."

Dr. Gamble guessed that a man could shoot somebody in twenty-five states and hide in twenty-three states. Dutch stared at the doctor. His thumbs gripped the Louis XIII chair hard enough to give it a royal headache. "What are you, some kind of smarty pants?" Dutch said savagely. "Did you hear this story before?"

The doctor assured Dutch he was only guessing. The old gangster seemed relieved. He stopped tugging at the machine gun barrel under his chair and resumed the conversation.

"Then I'm in Detroit in '27 when I hear about what's-his-name, the guy in the plane, the Lone Eagle."

"Lindbergh," Dr. Gamble said.

Dutch glared at his visitor. "You absolutely sure you never heard this story?" His right thumb spelled "murder one" in the dust on an end table.

Dr. Gamble swallowed nervously. He explained that he was anxious to hear about Dutch's non-running experiences. He tried to avoid glancing at his host's left thumbnail, which was painted with scenes from *Little Caesar*.

"Anyway," Dutch continued, a suspicious tone in his voice,

"I'm in Detroit waiting for your buddy Lindbergh. But the joke's on me because it turns out he was flying to Paris. So as not to waste my time in Detroit, some guy asked me to do a little job for him. After that I had to run someplace where the government boys couldn't lay a hand on me, someplace where I could getta hold of that good north-of-the-border booze, someplace where I could make Eskimo love, someplace—"

"Canada, huh?" Dr. Gamble said. He should have known better. Witnesses report that Dutch leaped from his chair and raced across the room.

"Dutch," the doctor said, "we're not supposed to be running."

Those were the doctor's final words: "We're not supposed to be running." The motto is available on key chains, sofa doilies, and leg irons.

Dutch (Crazy Thumbs) Klenzer was found guilty of doctor-slaughter and of hiring a lawyer who resembled Raymond Burr. He is currently awaiting execution. A capital idea. Non-Runners International is well rid of this old reprobate who has promised "to run the last mile."

14

Non-Running and Non-Being: The Totality of the Whole

George Shoeshine, who was often called the non-running dentist or the non-runners' guru or the non-runners' philosopher, or, occasionally, the nut from New Jersey, has inspired countless non-runners with his writings and his personal example.

As his many devoted readers know, Dr. Shoeshine did not

begin serious non-running until after his death at the age of sixty-three. Despite this handicap, he soon began eclipsing records set by dead people much younger than he. He has come to specialize in the difficult competitive area of lying quietly with absolutely no movement of any kind. However, he is versatile, and also enjoys decomposing. His many books on behavior in the bathroom received critical acclaim. He did not limit himself to brushing and flossing, the area of his expertise and training, but ventured fully into showering and shaving, toenail-clipping, and even the elimination of bodily wastes. (Dr. Shoeshine never shrank from controversial subjects just because some people might be squeamish about them.)

His ideas on bathrooms opened to non-runners a vital new area into which non-running could be expanded. For it was Dr. Shoeshine who first realized that the bathroom, with its small size and invariable clutter, was the ideal place to not run in. As a result, bathroom use in America increased dramatically.

In this chapter from his last and most personal book, Dr. Shoeshine Sits Down and Talks Serious Bathroom, *he discusses dental care, but not merely from the standpoint of technique, as is so often the case. Instead, Dr. Shoeshine plunges the non-running reader into a brisk examination of the philosophical basis of dental care and is able to impart the profound sense of joy that dental care brought to his own oral life. Also, he is able to work in the thousands of quotations he habitually jotted down on tiny pieces of paper and stuck in his ears for future reference.*

When I brush, I am a genius. For that moment, I am Michelangelo under the Sistine ceiling. I am Picasso cubed. I am Warhol in the supermarket seeking transcendence in the soup aisle. I am Shakespeare sonneting to beat the band. I am the son of Newton and Galileo, and Murray the K.

But off the brush, all changes. Then I am a hapless little creep with a big nose. I am mean, cheap, and sarcastic. I am cowardly and ugly and a molester of small children. I wet my pants.

On the other hand, though, I'm willing to blab absolutely everything about myself in print. I get points for vulnerability. In this I am not unique. I am exactly like Kierkegaard, Kant, Rimsky-Korsakov, Grover Cleveland Alexander, and Paul Muni. Emerson was like that, too. He once said, "All the talking I do, it makes me tired just to listen." That's Tony Emerson, fellow I knew in dental school.

But Proust had Emerson's number. That's Marcel Proust, fellow I met in Paris while taking a nap. "Ideas," wrote Proust, "make all the difference. Ideas and a high-interest savings account." I first read that when I was six. I knew then that my destiny was different from everyone else's in my family. They were all Negroes, whereas I was a white kid. "First," said Blake, "understand who you are. After that, you can get a bite to eat." I will not apologize, therefore, for my compulsion to brush my teeth.

Brushing is a total experience. No, strike that. Brushing is *the* total experience. Some people gain pleasure from eating good food, climbing mountains, or having sex with several people at once. I prefer pain and suffering. Pain cleanses. Suffering saves. What I do, I start at the gumline with the brush held at a 45-degree angle, remembering the advice of Tolstoy. I never read Tolstoy, but I saw the movie. "Come down hard," Tolstoy said, "until it hurts." To which Turgenev wittily replied, "Is that so?" The blood that seeps from my gums is just the external symbol of my will. My brush is its servant; my teeth the stars witnessing from the dark void of space.

Yes, I am a brusher. Deny it and I bristle. *I am a brusher.* Years ago, that statement would have meant nothing to me or to anyone else. It would be like the time Ortega y Gasset listened to a lecture by Tielhard de Chardin and commented, "I can't understand French." Today I know better. My body knows who I am. My teeth know the brush is coming. They lie in orderly rows, waiting. The brusher doesn't brush because he worries about dirty teeth. No. He brushes to fulfill himself and to become the person he is capable of becoming once he thinks he knows who he wishes to become.

To outsiders this may seem unnatural. The months spent locked in a steamy little bathroom. The vast amounts of money spent on toothpaste and brushes and floss. The constantly sore wrist. The bloody spittle splattering the white porcelain. The truth is, the brusher is not like other people. To use Ernest Borgnine's expression, his mouth is his cathedral, his tongue his altar, his teeth the outboard motor of his soul.

For when I brush I am a wrathful god and I am also an entreating supplicant. One is myself and the other is my truth. My self prays to my truth and my self answers. And the answer is the truth itself. I feel the truth and I know the truth and I take it and fling it back in my own face. I feel its force as a lash and I bow my head into the sink and say, "Thank you, Lord." And I answer, "You're welcome." Then both of us say, "Amen."

I am not a particularly religious man. My ex-wife liked to say I was a schizophrenic with messianic delusions. What can you expect? She is a non-brusher. A shallow person who doesn't understand. What's more, she has excessive plaque. I had to get rid of her. Her biting sarcasm set my teeth on edge. She didn't understand my needs. A brusher needs solitude. He needs to feel the wind in his gums. I cut her up in tiny pieces with my dental tools and I flushed her. Don't tell anyone—this is between you and me. I am a humble man, a modest man. But I know my duty. When someone sins, they must be punished. This is what I told Moses on that windy mountaintop so many years ago. "You're the boss," Moses sayeth at the time. Bearded guy with a robe. "Damn straight," I replied. It's as true today as it was then. I showed Moses the right way. Start at the gumline and bring it down to the edge of the tooth. He was good, too. Damned good. But the rest of them screwed it up, of course.

Brushing is a peak experience. It transcends. When the soft round tufts touch lightly against the enamel it is as if the first rays of the rising sun were breaking over the vast Pacific. All is fresh. All is new. Every tooth I brush is my first. Every thrust a new beginning. Each time I whip the floss through a lower molar and flick the food particles across space to collide with my mirror, I am reborn. I see everything as though for the first time. I see what St. Augustine saw when I revealed to him a vision of Sonny and Cher. He said, "What in hell is that?" And I replied, "That's the future, Auggie, and watch your language around me. Show some respect." He sulked off to ponder.

I only mixed with the best. Guys who never said anything quotable I didn't bother with. I kept a notebook with me and jotted down any bon mots I heard. Oscar Wilde, he was the best. But, you know, Attila the Hun was fast with a quip. I figured some day when I got around to it I'd put them all together and publish a book of quotes, but that son of a bitch Bartlett beat me to it. But I found another use for them all. I quote them to myself as I brush. All I do now is brush. "Brusha brusha brusha," as Chaucer said. I'm in here twenty-four hours a day now, working up a hell of a shine.

And reflecting. Reflecting in all senses of the word. You could look into my teeth and see your own soul mirrored there. That is, you could if I let you. But you can't come in here. Not in my bathroom. My bathroom is for me alone. Sorry. "A man's bathroom is a man's bathroom, no two ways about it," said Santayana.

Do you know that people once actually thought they were supposed to brush their teeth side to side? Can you believe it? This was the dark past. Man has come far. He will come farther. He will overcome plaque. He will beat caries. His enamel will gleam. And I will be there to help and guide him— and her, for I am no sexist. I am watching, have no fear. By my mouth shall ye know me. By my gaping maw. "Hi, Maw," as Whistler said. And only when this has been accomplished shall I have my final rest and my teeth grind no more. Only then will I unclench and set the choppers floating in a glass of water on my night table. Only then will I sigh and say my last goob nighp.

15 🐢

The Nine Greatest
Non-Running Movies—
Plus Three

The movies have long been a favorite of non-runners. From the earliest days of silent films, when quick-turning the handle on primitive cameras gave the illusion of running (with none of the anguish), non-runners have considered Hollywood a strong ally.

Consider the following:

How do you buy a movie ticket? You wait on lines that may not move for hours.

What happens after you finally buy your ticket? You wait on the ticket-holders' line.

How do you watch movies? Sitting down.

What do you do when the movie ends and you're late for an appointment? Won't you have to run then? Not a chance. You're part of a big crowd stuck in a teeny little aisle. You aren't going anywhere for a while.

Non-runners chuckle at the runner who couldn't wait for the opening of *Run Silent, Run Deep*. He was first on line, first in the theater, and first to gnash his teeth when he discovered he was watching a film about submarines.

We have dozens of films on our all-time favorite list and choosing the Top Ten wasn't easy. Nine, however, was a snap. You may disagree. Then again, you may not give a damn. After all, isn't that what non-running is all about?

STALAG 17 (1953) *William Holden.* Fun and games in the German countryside. Some prisoners, though, are unhappy about their accommodations. In the movie's only depressing scene, they run away.

CITIZEN KANE (1941) *Orson Welles.* A publisher builds a big house and nobody comes to visit him. He dies because of poor circulation. His wife later tells her story to a newsreel company. This greatest of all American films contains no running sequences. Not a foot.

STRANGERS ON A TRAIN (1951) Two men meet. One plays tennis and one doesn't. One has a wife he wants to get rid of, and the other isn't too crazy about his backhand. As in all his films, Alfred Hitchcock makes a brief non-running appearance.

TWELVE ANGRY MEN (1957) *Henry Fonda.* High-jinx in the jury box. But these men have to decide the fate of a murder suspect. Did he or didn't he? You won't leave your chair as you watch twelve men reach a decision without leaving their table. A lot of yelling.

KING KONG (1933) A financially troubled city is no place for this big ape. He gets lousy reviews as the top banana in a nightclub act and blames everyone but himself. He finally finds a date who can put up with his monkeyshines and takes her to the top of the Empire State Building. But he's too much of a boob to enjoy the view. He's such a smart guy he doesn't use the elevator on the way down. He reminds us of a lot of runners we know.

LIFEBOAT (1944) *Alfred Hitchcock* scores again, cleverly setting this entire movie in a lifeboat on the open sea, thus drastically restricting any opportunities for running. It was rumored during the making of the film that Tallulah Bankhead tried to run from one side of the boat to the other, despite cries from fellow actors to "Sit down, you're rocking the boat." She finally desisted after Hitchcock spanked her severely.

THE BLOB (1958) *Steve McQueen.* This film, in which a huge slithery amoeba-like organism terrorizes a midwestern community, was a favorite non-running movie of the fifties. Blobs, of course, cannot run, or even walk quickly, but can only pulsate and hope for rides from passing truck drivers. The Blob itself came to symbolize the values of the sedentary life, and the film's popularity resulted in higher sales for kitchen and bathroom sponges.

L'AVVENTURA (1961) *Michelangelo Antonioni* is considered the greatest of all non-running directors. Antonioni movies not only feature superb non-running, they render virtually all action non-existent, and uncannily produce the effect of watching a still photograph.

THE SKY ABOVE, THE MUD BELOW (1961) This documentary portrays the daily life of a primitive tribe in New Guinea which has not yet advanced far enough in the path of human development to have discovered non-running. Technically a pre-non-running film, it effectively foreshadows the tribe's evolutionary progress toward non-running through symbolic actions, such as the tribe's fascination with the cameraman's sleeping bag. They attempt to stuff him in it, boil, and serve.

The following non-running films will soon be at a theater near you.

DRACULA'S TAX LAWYER The Count moves to Switzerland and meets a banker's daughter at an all-night disco in Zurich. He asks her for a date. In the movie's most memorable sequence, Dracula promises the girl's mother they'll be home before sunup. When it looks as if they aren't going to make it, the girl begins to run. She reaches home well after sunrise, and her mother is worried sick. Dracula comes back that night and the mother accuses him of being a wolf. He tries to explain that she has him mixed up with Lon Chaney, Jr., but mom isn't buying. Dracula is crushed. To forget the girl, he enters the Geneva-to-Basel marathon and sucks the blood of the last twenty-five finishers. The film ends with runners everywhere sporting the newest look: two small holes in the side of their sneakers.

THE ROAD TO NOWHERE In this last film in their Road series, Bing and Bob play a pair of animal trainers named Bong and Bib. They become stranded on an island in the Pacific when their light plane is forced down by the energy crisis. Searching for a restaurant that will allow them to use the bathroom *and* make phone calls, Bong and Bib are surrounded by cannibals. Bong suggests they kidnap the chief's near-naked daughter and make a run for it. Bib is afraid the censors will come after them. In the film's most memorable scene, the censors don't move a muscle.

ROCKY MEETS GODZILLA   Here's Marlon Brando as a high school principal who has never been west of Newark. When a strike closes his school he jumps into a cab and asks to be taken to a massage parlor. The cabbie makes a wrong turn and lets Brando off in Bar Harbor, Maine. In the movie's most memorable scene, Brando refuses to tip the driver. Brando begins swimming back to Manhattan and reaches Pier 48 just as the *Queen Mary* is pulling in. Later that afternoon, a long-shoreperson is being told there won't be any work that day because of a collision between the *Queen Mary* and a high school principal. The longshoreperson shrieks. Her mother was on the *Queen*, returning from the Geneva-to-Basel marathon. She waits on the dock while the authorities check to see if there are any survivors.

In the film's final shot, Brando is floating inside a life preserver. He reaches into the back of his shirt and pulls out a fish. He and the fish exchange smiles and we realize, as the camera moves closer, that he isn't wearing a life preserver after all; it's just more Brando.

16

How Non-Runners Cope

The importance of not running every day can't be measured. All too often people put it off until the next day. And then till that night. Until finally, after a second act intermission, it's later that same evening in Lord Faversham's study.

Nobody ever said not running on a regular schedule was

going to be easy. But we feel no sympathy for those silver bells and cockleshells who skip a day. Skipping, as practiced in this country by seven-year-old boys and girls, is more objectionable than all-out running.

The beauty of non-running is that it can be done anywhere. Anytime. Wholesale.

A non-runner of our acquaintance returned from a trip to Russia where he was guest speaker at the Moscow monthly meeting of Nyet-Jogski Nyet-Runski Nyet-Trotski. Comparing notes after the meeting he found that non-runners the world over have the same highs, the same lows, and don't mess with Mr. In Between.

At a performance of the famed Bolshoi Ballet he quickly discovered that a dedicated non-runner could sleep through an evening of Bolshoi with no more effort than it takes to snooze through a twilight doubleheader. The Bolshoi's energetic tympanist, in fact, was no match for your average scorecard vendor.

We hear these stories about people who find a way to ignore each day as it comes and, if awake, we nod and smile. F. Scott Fitzgerald, who is best remembered for *The Great Gatsby*— a novel that proved you don't need a lot of running scenes to sell a few copies—once wrote that the rich are different from you and me. We hate to argue with a guy who isn't around to defend himself, but we think Scotty must never have had the pleasure of knowing Thruck Pumpernickel. Old Thruck is sure one dedicated non-runner. And the point is, he doesn't have to dedicate himself to much of anything these days because his Uncle Julius was sharp enough to invent the Excuse.

Uncle Julius, by the way, is still tinkering in his laboratory. He came out recently, disturbing that part of the afternoon which Thruck devotes exclusively to not running, and began mouthing off about a new improved product.

"I've got the perfect Excuse," Uncle Julius said. He tapped his fingers against it, producing the familiar whining noise.

"Sounds like the same old Excuse to me," Thruck said. He looked at his watch. If the old man didn't leave soon, Thruck knew he'd have to non-run in the evening to make up for the time he was losing now. He punched his pillowcase, hoping Uncle Julius would take the hint. No, the old man wasn't buying it.

"Where did you ever hear a better Excuse than this one?" his uncle asked.

"I'll tell you the truth," Thruck snapped, "It's getting to the point where all your Excuses sound alike to me."

Had he gone too far? The old man was clearly hurt. Tough ankles, Thruck thought, but a non-runner always says what's on his mind. One more nasty insult and he felt certain his uncle would leave.

"The fact is," Thruck said, clapping his hands over both ears, "that Excuse is a dime a dozen."

Thruck was unprepared for the old man's reaction. "Wonderful," Julius shouted. "My boy, you're a genius, a slice off the old Pumpernickel. We haven't had an economy product since I invented the Excuse that isn't worth the paper it's written on. Dime-a-Dozen Excuses will make us a fortune. Pretty soon everybody will be using them. Do you think Nixon will endorse them?"

Thruck threw up his hands and went back into the laboratory with his uncle. He would have to forget about not running until later that night. "Look, Uncle," Thruck said as they disappeared into the lab, "I'll help you this one more time but—"

"Not to worry." The old man was cackling. "I promise this is the last Excuse you'll hear from me."

The truth is, Thruck's non-running schedule was badly disrupted. He tried to double up the next day and had to rush through lunch. Got him good and sick too, pretty much the same thing that would happen to you or me. See what we mean, Scott?

The veteran non-runner faces obstacles daily. The newcomer must beware. Here are some of our favorite obstacles:

THE SURLY BARTENDER

You have decided to not run for the afternoon at a pub that has recently opened in the neighborhood. The challenge of new

Roland La Bomba sprints through subway turnstiles after taking wrong turn in 1976 New York Marathon and completing most of the 26-mile course underground. La Bomba would have finished third in race but was arrested by pursuing transit police shortly before he neared the tape and was charged with creating a potentially ridiculous situation.

Non-runners in Oregon sprint toward finish in marathon tree-leaning doubles event.

terrain is one you have been looking forward to. Unfortunately the bartender has misplaced his martini onions and is in a foul mood. He is slamming drinks, flicking his wet bar rag at imaginary roaches, and playing Teresa Brewer records. Non-running is becoming uncomfortable but you can't leave. You're too dedicated. God, what a lousy afternoon. Buy another round.

SUPERMARKET EXPRESS CHECKOUT LINES

All you wanted was a package of chocolate-chip cookies, a box of marshmallow choco-puffs, a cinnamon-nut crunch bar, and a tube of skin-care cream. Juggling them in your hands you get on the express checkout line. The woman in front of the line has been discovered to have eleven items, one more than the express checkout maximum. The nursery school dropout who rings up the sales refuses to deal with the woman and her eleven purchases. "I know my limits," he keeps saying. The woman insists she got on line with ten items. She swears that someone slipped the oregano into her basket when she wasn't looking. You glance helplessly at the cash registers on either side of you. Whole nations have gone through while your express line stands still.

The experienced non-runner shops at four p.m.

PRIME-TIME TELEVISION

The schedules for the major networks have been released for next season. The new shows include an adventure series featuring three sexy grandmothers, an adventure series featuring three sexy experts in forensic medicine, an adventure series featuring three sexy police dogs, a mini-series drawn from a book of favorite police recipes, a situation comedy about the kidnapping of an Italian premier, a sports show with teams of celebrities who play tennis with rotten plums, David Susskind in a two-hour talk show *without* guests, a situation comedy about three sexy economists and their wacky adventures as they try to stem the rate of inflation.

The rest of the schedule consists of thirty minutes of local weather and three sexy anchorpeople visiting their hairdressers. It's enough to make any non-runner think about turning off his set. Without television, the non-runner is left with little to amuse himself. He may find himself picking up a book. And by then, since the only books published will be about running, he might be overwhelmed by running propaganda. Beware! Turn that set back on. Try to find something you like. Commercials, station breaks, public television, football halftimes, anything.

17

Non-Running and the Athlete

Can an athlete also be a non-runner? Is it ethical for athletes to non-run? These are questions we were recently asked by a major-league umpire with an epistemological turn of mind.

Paradoxical as it may seem, an athlete can also be a full-time non-runner. The key to avoiding a conflict here lies in carefully choosing which athletic events you participate in. To illustrate, here are three top athletes of our acquaintance, who are also total non-runners:

Toby Schwenk: coxswain, varsity crew, University of Arizona. Toby Schwenk has led UA to two Southwest Conference championships, yet has not run a step since junior high school. Typically, he sits quietly in the back of the boat, counting time and taking total responsibility for steering. After their big win against archrival New Mexico State, the UA crew tossed Toby in the water in the traditional gesture of celebration. So dedicated was Toby to non-running, he refused even to swim for shore. The university recently dedicated its new field house to his memory.

Scientists predict that non-running will domi-
nate all sports by the next century. Already,
sophisticated alternatives to running are appear-
ing on athletic fields across the country. In a
recent college baseball game, Harvard (top)
was beaten by MIT, 8–7.

Dominico Malanango: bobsledder, Italian Olympic team. Dominico's sport, like Toby Schwenk's, requires him to sit down. In fact, the first thing a bobsledder is taught is, never stand up while the sled is in motion. Dominico is good at sitting down, one of the world's best. Concentration is all-important, he says. He concentrates on not falling off. Another guy does the steering and Dominico holds on to his back, leaning either left or right, depending on which way the sled is turning. To keep in shape during the summer months, Dominico, who lives in Rome, jumps on the back of buses and hangs on as long as possible.

Bart Shotover, harness driver: Bart has won over three million dollars in the past five years by sitting in a little cart and staring at the rear end of a horse. "It's a strange view," he says, "but you get used to it. Except for the sudden stops." Bart sensibly figures there's no point in his running, since the horse is much faster and is willing to carry both of them.

18

The Rape of the Foot

One of the most unfortunate by-products of the recent running boom has been the glorification of the lowly foot, an organ previously considered obscene.

Throughout Western civilization the foot has, from the first, been kept strictly covered up and out of sight. Soon after its discovery in what is now Syria, the foot was encased in a garment unlike any other: the strong, rigid restraining device known as the shoe (derived from the ancient Sumerian word *shoobidoo*, literally meaning "big bony thing that goes clop-clop"). The shoe's tough, boxlike construction, often reinforced with nails, was designed to ensure the continued imprisonment of the surly and often rebellious foot. But even this was not enough, and humanity was soon forced to invent the sock.

Early man feared the foot's animal-like power, its pungent odor, its whimsical habit of contracting bizarre and annoying diseases, and its inclination to kick, a form of violence engaged in by no other limb. The Visigoths often defeeted their vanquished foes, believing that this would assuage the easily offended gods.

The artists of the Renaissance insisted on keeping the foot in the lower half of their paintings to symbolize its baseness and insensitivity. Philosophers, too, have always looked down on the feet. It was Aristotle who first postulated that because the foot is the organ furthest from the brain, it is the least intelligent. Erasmus, who was said to suffer horribly from fallen arches, attacked the foot as "a coarse, unfeeling terminus; a collector of dirt; a mere pod devoid of wit or splendor." St. Thomas Aquinas referred to the feet as "dumb things," and Kant once wrote: "Foot, what is it? It's not a head, I know that much."

In the Victorian era, the word "foot" was itself considered shocking and never mentioned in mixed company. Euphemisms such as "shoe-filler," "double-Ls," "stem," and "pedestal" were substituted. Foot suppression went so far that it spawned vast numbers of fetishists who frequented specialized brothels where reluctant barefoot contessas were forced to toe-dance on their faces.

The advent of modern science has only confirmed many of the ancient prejudices. Today it is known, for instance, that the foot really started out as a hand. It contains not only the same number of digits, but also the same number of bones—twenty-six. But the foot apparently retrogressed through evolutionary laziness to the point where its toes lost all their clutching and grabbing abilities and became virtually useless appendages, depriving us of much-needed dexterity below the waist. Think what we could do with a fully aware and operative foot. Why, a person would be able to dial a phone, change channels on the

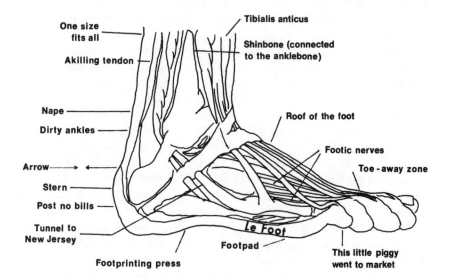

One size
fits all

Akilling tendon

Tibialis anticus

Shinbone (connected
to the anklebone)

Nape

Dirty ankles

Roof of the foot

Footic nerves

Toe - away zone

Arrow

Stern

Post no bills

Tunnel to
New Jersey

Le Foot

Footpad

This little piggy
went to market

Footprinting press

The Foot (life-sized)

TV set, write a postcard, and blow his nose all at once, if not for the tragic foot-dragging of those two sorry loafers which now lie limply in the feetal position.

Despite all this evidence of pedal inferiority, today we suddenly see the foot paraded everywhere before us. Wherever you look you see tapping toes, triumphal arches, high heels, and redeemed soles, tripping unshod and unashamed. Bare feet. You see them leering from the pages of slick magazines, their fat, pudgy pink toes wriggling lasciviously. No longer are feet anchored to floors. You see them draped casually atop a desk, sticking belligerently out of trouser legs, sailing into the rib cage of a Kung-Fu enthusiast, or passing a bar of soap to a reclining bather. People of all ages are encouraged to go shoeless to the seashore today, despite the dangers of sharp shells and beer cans, a situation ripe for tragedy. Entire books devoted to the feet are being published and even books on subjects entirely unrelated are increasingly filled with footnotes.

Responsibility for all this madness must be laid squarely at the feet of the running enthusiasts. Unable to avoid the damaging admission that the one indispensable element of their beloved sport was this singularly unlovable locomotor, the running pedagogues decided to put their best foot forward: They launched a propaganda crusade to upgrade the foot and make it acceptable—even attractive—to the public. The campaign's masterstroke to date has been the transformation of the sneaker (or "running shoe," as they insist on calling it) into a gaily colored bon-bon, all in electric blues, fiery reds, and zippy stripes. Unlike the drab beiges and blacks long used in traditional footwear to draw attention away from the ungainly member, these hot numbers proclaim that feet, far from being pedestrian, are exciting, sexy, and fun to be with.

Unfortunately, they aren't. Those brightly shod runners have feet of clay. Despite their desperate efforts at image-upgrading, the ironic truth is that running is the worst thing that can befall a foot. With all its drawbacks, the human foot, left to itself, is capable of leading a useful and constructive life. It will never soar, of course. It has no imagination. But its one unquestioned virtue is sturdiness. Most non-runners know that by keeping their feet off the ground and out of action as much as possible, they can get up to a century of wear out of them. But runners abuse their feet. At the same time they place themselves in a state of total dependence on them. This is an act of unparalleled silliness. Because given half a chance, a foot will let you down.

The foot is subject to diseases and injuries not found in any other part of the body. Can you imagine a face with bunions or an abdominal corn? Never! A foot can also catch calluses, blisters, warts, ingrown toenails, sprains, fungus infections, spurs, clubfoot, "black toenail" (blood blisters), fallen arches, shin splints, tendonitis and, worst of all, lopsidedness.

Few people are aware that after heart disease and cancer, foot ailments are the third most crippling health problem in the U.S., a fact which gives new significance to the phrase, "He has one foot in the grave."

Whatever potential or existing ailments your feet are subject to, running will do nothing but aggravate and intensify them. The average person takes about five thousand steps during an hour's run and every one of them is a kick in the foot. No wonder runners are always suffering injuries. No wonder their feet are killing them. They are being trampled underfoot.

Chief beneficiaries of this vast sea of pain are the nation's 7,500 podiatrists, who now earn an average of $42,000 annually and are quite thankful for the nation's runners. For it is the runners who foot the bill. Except for mailmen, non-runners contribute little to the welfare of podiatrists. Non-runners keep their dogs up and their pedicure tab down. They follow the four cardinal rules of foot care and, as a result, most boast a pair of pods as tender as a newborn hush puppy.

THE FOUR RULES OF FOOT

1. Raise your feet higher than your head at least three times a day. This allows your feet to "breathe." Also, in warm weather they need to expand. And, occasionally, they need to scream.

2. Treat your toes to a decent tickle at least once every day. A tickled toe is a happy toe, and as the toe goes, so goes the foot.
3. Always wear your shoes to work. This is especially important in colder climates.
4. Discipline your feet if necessary, but never in front of other feet. Feet are easily embarrassed. And never use force on a recalcitrant foot. A stern lecture should suffice.

If everyone followed these four rules instead of sticking their feet in sneakers and hijacking them four times around the park each day, then it may eventually become possible for the feet to once again resume their rightful place beneath society.

19

The Spread of Non-Running

We stepped into a cab the other day and were pleasantly surprised to find a sign that read "Thank You for Not Running." The license on the dashboard told us that the driver's name was Martin Greenery. We immediately struck up a conversation.

"How do you find people reacting to your request?"

"Let me tell you something," he said. "That ain't no request. Originally I had up there 'Run Here and I Break Your Kneecaps.' My wife's the diplomat in the family. She thinks you can get more with kind words than you can with a claw hammer. I told her I'd try it her way for two weeks."

"And if it didn't work?"

"I'd break *her* kneecaps."

Greenery went on to explain that a number of drivers met at

Headlights, New York's only topless garage, for weekly discussions on politics and the arts. It was during a brisk debate on what certain passengers will do when a driver's back is turned that the subject of running in cabs was brought up.

All agreed that the practice had to be discouraged. The atmosphere of a cab after a runner leaves its confines will almost certainly have an unpleasant effect on the next passenger. The drivers have discovered that the only way to counteract the unpleasantness is to fill the back seat with cheap cigar smoke. This often results in the driver's being unable to see his next fare. One such driver came home recently and was greeted by his wife's favorite question: "Did anyone famous ride with you today?"

"Who knows?" the cabbie answered. "The cigar smoke was so thick in the back because of those damn runners I couldn't tell Zbigniew Brzezinski from Darth Vader."

Recently, Greenery said, chuckling at the memory, a woman stepped into his cab wearing a sweatsuit and sneakers and carrying a stopwatch. "Jack LaLoo"s Health Spa and step on it," she said.

The driver eyed her suspiciouly. "You some kind of runner?" he said, easing the cab into the flow of midtown traffic where it remained for three weeks.

"She admitted she was a runner," Greenery said. "So I made sure she saw the sign. So she says she would never think of running in cabs. That she'd be afraid of what runners call 'Yellow Menace.'

"Well, there was no trouble until we turn on Madison. Then I think I hear something like 'Plonk.' "

"Plonk?" we repeated. "What does Plonk tell you?"

"Not a whole lot," Greenery admitted. "Plonk by itself isn't nothing to worry about. Maybe she's matching half-dollars with herself and one falls on the floor—Plonk. Maybe she's one of them dames wears tinsel freckles and when one of them falls off—Plonk. But you gotta remember this babe was wearing that sweatsuit. And 'Plonk' can just as easily be the sound of one foot running."

We marveled at Greenery's shrewdness.

Long-distance runners often suffer toe loss. Here Dave Pringlitz tries desperately to refasten big toe that dropped off during 1974 Boston Marathon.

"So, anyway, after I hear the first Plonk I start listening pretty hard for another one. I'm waiting for a light on Thirty-fourth Street and there it was."

"Plonk?"

"No, the Empire State Building. Yeah, Plonk, absolutely, no doubt. Just like I'm repeating it to you. PLONK! Real loud. She must have been wearing some real cheap sneaker. Pretty soon there's a couple of them. Plonk, Plonk, Plonk. So I know I gotta do something. I look in my mirror but all I can see is that she's sitting on the seat like nothing's wrong. They're pretty quick, some of these runners. We're trying to get mirrors put in, floor to ceiling, so we can see their shoes. Maybe my grandkids will live to see that day.

"Anyway we're rolling up Madison and she can't help herself. Plonk, Plonk, Plonk, Plonk, Plonk, Plonk, Plonk, Plonk, Plonk, Plonk—sounded like a mini-marathon. So I pull the cab to the curb and tell her to Plonk the hell out.

"Naturally, she starts crying. She says she's sorry—she couldn't help herself. She apologizes because she knows it's a filthy habit and she's sorry about what it might do to unborn generations. She says it's been hell on her since they prohibited running in movie theaters and on elevators. She took a flight from New York to Paris the other day, and the only seat left was in the non-running section. She had to lock herself in the bathroom to run and when she came out, all sweaty, every guy in the plane was staring at her.

"Hey, Martin Greenery got feelings like anybody else. I let her get back in the cab when she promised she wouldn't run anymore. And she didn't. Gave me a nice tip, too. But then I had to spend it all on cheap cigars. By the time I picked up my next fare the back seat looked like the London waterfront."

"Did the passenger mind?"

"Nah, he was a real decent guy. He said he was a doctor and had twelve kids. Since he was a doc I figured I'd ask him what he thought of my sign. He said that if I felt that strongly about it I ought to write a book. So I told him that what I'd rather do was kill a few runners. He said that he knew lots of books that were doing just that. Best of all nobody could figure out a motive and there might be a lucrative paperback sale."

The cab hummed along Fifth Avenue and Greenery whistled, totally oblivious to where we asked him to take us. "Yeah, maybe I will write a book," he said. He patted a humidor of El Dankos on his front seat. "Yeah, I just might do that."

20

How to Talk to a Runner

Non-runners often have difficulty understanding runners. This is because runners have a language of their own. Fortunately, however, one need not become a runner in order to learn this obscure tongue. Although Runnese sounds complex at first, it actually consists of fewer than twenty-five words and phrases, at least nineteen of which refer to some type of injury. When these words are grafted onto conventional English sentences, what results is the illusion that one is holding a normal conversation. Once mastered, this vocabulary will allow the non-runner to communicate with runners (although why he would want to is beyond us).

The following passage, a conversation recently overheard between two competitors struggling up a steep incline in the annual Himalayan Marathon, contains every single running expression known to footkind. Running words are indicated by numbers in parentheses. Definitions follow. Study the passage well, memorize it if necessary, and soon you, too, will be able to run off at the mouth.

FRED: How's it going?
JED: Pretty good.
FRED: Nice racing weather up here.

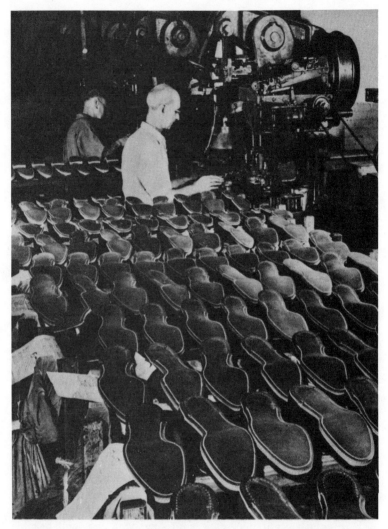

Runners suffering from "black toe" and other foot breakdowns hang upside down on racks in public foot clinic in St. Louis waiting for massive injections of anesthetic administered by giant rotary hypodermic engines. Hanging causes blood to leave feet, thus helping to alleviate pressure.

JED: Sure is.

FRED: Your chondromalacia patella(1) giving you any trouble?

JED: Nah. Got an orthotic(2) for it.

FRED: Oh, yeah?

JED: That's right.

FRED: My plantar fasciitis(3) was acting up a mile back, but it seems okay now.

JED: That so?

FRED: Hey, you know Ted Franzese?

JED: Short guy in Nike Waffle Trainers(4)?

FRED: That's him.

JED: What about him?

FRED: Passed him on the last hill. Poor bastard was flat on his back in the road, bleeding from the quad(5) and hamstring(6).

JED: No kidding.

FRED: That's right. Probably too much carbo-loading(7) last night.

JED: Yeah, he was really putting away the fettucini Alfredo. I warned him. Those Nepalese guys don't know how to cook it right.

FRED: Maybe he just hit the wall(8).

JED: You kidding? After two miles?

FRED: Last week I saw him out on some LSDs(9) and fartleks(10).

JED: LSDs(9) and what?

FRED: Fartleks(10). Looked like he was in good shape then. He was having some shin splint(11) trouble but nothing like this.

JED: I never liked the son of a bitch anyway.

FRED: Me neither.

JED: Say, is that a Yeti(12) on that ridge over there?

FRED: Naw, that's just Willie Gottshalk. Idaho Track Club. Boy, you must be getting an epinephrine(13) rush.

JED: I don't use that stuff. I'm on LSD(9).

FRED: Hey, look at that. Gottshalk just fell off the ridge. Must be about a six-hundred-foot drop.

JED: Now that's what I call a peak experience(14).

FRED: No more Magic Sixes(15) for him, that's for sure.

JED: Talk about hitting the wall(16).

FRED: Yeah, tough luck. Well, it's been nice chatting but I got to pull ahead now and win this race. Not bad for a guy with Morton's foot(17), huh?

JED: You'll fade in about(18) miles. Then I'll take you.

FRED: Fat chance, buddy. You're a disgrace to aerobics(19), you know that?

JED: Eat my dust, jerk. By the time you're getting your third wind(20), I'll be back in the locker room with a brew.

FRED: Up your triglycerides(21), pal.

THE DEFINITIONS

(1) Runner's knee.

(2) A plastic insert placed in sneakers by podiatrists to correct foot and leg problems.

(3) A pain in the heel.

(4) A form of sneaker.

(5) Some sort of leg muscle.

(6) Some sort of tendon.

(7) Eating large amounts of carbohydrate before a race is a trendy diet endorsed by some runners.

(8) The moment when your energy is totally exhausted and you feel unable to move another step.

(9) Long Slow Distance running, a form of training.

(10) Swedish for "speed play"; a freestyle, indefinite, "fun" running workout.

(11) Pain in the shins.

(12) A very tall, hairy runner found only at high altitudes.

(13) A hormone released by exercise, thought by some doctors to be the basis for happy feeling in the body.

(14) A moment when you feel completely at one with the world and transcend all conflicts as you finally become your own potential.

(15) A series of warm-up calisthenics for runners.

Visitors to this shop located on Beverly Hills' Million-Dollar Mile
are amazed at the variety of shoes offered by storekeeper Denzil
Wicker. Denzil shod every competitor in the first and only
San Andreas Marathon, a financial disaster. The sponsors blamed
Denzil, claiming he provided galoshes to runners he bet against.
"Let me tell you about those phonies from San Andreas," Denzil
said. "It's never their fault."

(16) A fall from six hundred feet or more which completely crushes the bones and destroys all internal organs.
(17) A condition in which the second toe is longer than the first toe.
(18) Eighteen.
(19) Exercises like running, biking, and swimming which allegedly promote the body's oxygen supply.
(20) A form of intestinal disturbance that often follows carboloading.
(21) A blood lipid.

21

Are Runners Boring?

You often hear people say that running and jogging are boring activities, indulged in by boring people, that lead to boring thoughts and boring conversations. Frankly, we feel that such characterizations are cheap and unfair. And so we offered space for rebuttal to the well-known writer/runner James X. Fizz, author of the distinguished book *The Complete Runaway Best Seller*. Mr. Fizz graciously sent us the following reply:

"Do I think runners are boring? Heck, no. Some of my best friends are runners, and we've had many wonderful, stimulating conversations, sometimes right in the middle of a run! What do we talk about? Well, we talk of many things. We talk about life itself, about its frustrations and its rewards, about its unpredictability—you know, like how one never knows what's waiting around the next bend of the road, and about how you have to take the good with the bad, but that however bad things may seem, there's always a silver lining.

"That's not all, either. We talk about sports and books and current events, too. Sometimes we even talk about sex! (Although not too much, because it seems to lower our times.) And quite often, we talk about our favorite movies and TV shows. Like I was out running with my wife the other day and she was telling me about this "Happy Days" she'd seen, where Ron Howard wins the big basketball game and becomes the school hero, right? So now he thinks he's such a hotshot that *he* tries to fix up the Fonz with a date. Can you imagine the guy's nerve? The Fonz! Well, anyway, I forget how it came out, but Fonzie really put him in his place and it was hysterical. Then I told her about this "Wild Kingdom" I was watching, where Marlon Perkins outwits a wily mother ostrich and tracks her to the nest and gets this fantastic closeup of the young ostriches hatching, okay? Then you see Marlon back in the studio, where he does this brilliant lead-in right into the Mutual of Omaha message, all about how you too should make sure you have a nest egg for a rainy day. Boy, it just knocked me out.

"So basically I just have to say that all this talk about runners being boring is nothing but a lot of crap, if you'll pardon my French."

22

Sex and the Single Non-Runner

This chapter was difficult to write. Non-runners, by nature, are rarely blowhards. Their accomplishments are personal triumphs, their yarns uncollected in hardcover, their advertisements for themselves usually hidden beneath the hemorrhoid cures. We asked thousands of non-runners if they were getting any, but they were too modest to reply in detail. All they did was grunt obscenely.

It was for these reasons that we felt we needed research assistants. Mr. Grossberger said he knew of a terrific research assistant on 48th Street and Eighth Avenue (the northwest corner). Mr. Ziegel, on the other hand, was hoping for a volunteer in his research. He said he had never paid for it and never would.

Our findings:

Runners will never admit it, but non-runners make better lovers. We proved this by sending a questionnaire to every runner in America. A great many of the envelopes came back stamped, "Damn Fool Too Busy Running To Pick Up His Mail." Or "Big Dummy Lost His Mailbox Key." Also, "Too Weak From Running To Open Envelope." Our favorite was stamped, "Return To Sender: Addressee Ran Out On Rent, Leaving Apartment a Mess, Toaster on Dark, Washing Machine on Spin, Banana Peels Everywhere."

Our questions:

1. Are you more interested in (A) running or (B) sex? Pick one.
2. If your answer is (A), what's your problem?
3. Do you run because you can't get any (B)?
4. Do you know stories about (A) and (B) that can be used in a book for general audiences?
5. Do you usually find yourself (A) in the park?
6. Or is (B) in the park your idea of a good time?
7. Do you seek (B) after (A)? Or do you take a shower? Or both?
8. Where do babies come from—(A) or (B)? No peeking at question one.
9. If you fell in love with a non-runner would you suggest a little (A)? How long do you think it would last?
10. Did you ever confuse (A) and (B)?

Violet Fitzgerald (bottom) *poses with princesses of her court after her selection as Miss Non-Runner of 1917. Winner was chosen after six finalists sat in front row of audience while judges paraded past them on runway.*

11. Have you ever noticed that when you are (A) by yourself your hair falls out?
12. Did you learn about (B) from X-rated films?
13. Do you find yourself (A) to the latest X-rated films?
14. Were you waiting for the right marathon before you had your first taste of (A)?
15. Did you feel clean after your initiation to (A)?
16. What was the longest you ever went without (A)? Without (B)?

The answers made us giggle. Dr. Comonna Myhaus, valedictorian of her Masters and Johnson class, did incredible work among runners and non-runners during her sixteenth summer at Camp Hickey. She was halfway through the Lollipop Division when the summer ended. "The non-runners," she reports, "were always my favorites. Pretty soon it got to where I could tell a runner from a non-runner in the dark."

It is often pointed out to us that the author of *Running and Being* is the father of twelve children. This is usually followed by an elbow into our ribs and a salacious chuckle. We are not impressed.

Our files are filled to overflowing with non-running fathers of fifteen, eighteen, twenty-one. King Zut, the non-running ruler of his island monarchy, Beezores (population, 63), is truly the father of his country.

We are continually bombarded by stories of runners who smash records only minutes after leaving their bedchambers, of athletes who say their performances are enhanced by lovemaking the night before a game. Our reply is: Where are the pictures? Play us the tapes. Show us the phone numbers.

Ty Cobb, the Georgia Peach, was said to have avoided lovemaking from the first day of spring training to the last out of the World Series. It is hardly a coincidence that he is remembered as the meanest man to ever play baseball.

As a starlet, Raquel W., a movie star who asked us not to use her full name, often ran in marathons. She had been told she would be noticed by producers who often scouted marathons to find new talent. After one such run, the 26 miles of

Paramount Studios (42,451 times around Francis Ford Coppola), she finally swore off.

"I guess I could see it coming," she said, giving us a few minutes on the set of her film, *I, Minnie Mouse.* She pointed to a scar on her left knee. "I got that in my first marathon but it didn't stop me. I ran in lots of marathons, probably some you never even heard of. Like the Death Valley Run, twenty-six miles through the desert where everybody had to carry their own water pitchers. And nobody had bigger jugs than I did. But do you think any producers gave me a tumble? Don't make me laugh.

"I ran twenty-six miles in the San Fernando Treadmill Marathon and nobody cared if I was coming or going. I said to myself, 'Raquel W., this is crazy. Running isn't helping your career.' Well, the first day I stopped, my agent got me an appointment with a non-running producer. My agent said there wasn't much chance I'd get a part in the guy's film but it couldn't hurt to visit his office.

"I got the part and my career took off. You think I'd be making this movie now"—she pulled at her mouse ears—"if I was still running? Forget it."

Before we left we asked if she had any advice for today's aspiring actresses. "You bet," she said. "Tell them to throw away their sneakers and forget everything they've heard about sweatsuits. Did you ever see Mamie Van Doren run? Or Clara Bow? Or Ida Lupino? 'Course not. And they didn't do too bad for themselves." She glanced at the set and spotted her co-star, Mickey Mouse. "I gotta get back," she said, pulling on her white gloves. "The big cheese is waiting."

We are reminded of the story about the traveling salesman who stopped at a farmhouse. He asked if he might stay the night while local mechanics tried to find his muffler. The farmer showed him to a bedroom. He then took him next door, where a well-endowed young woman wearing a shortie nightgown was singing, "Teach Me Tonight."

"This here's my daughter," the farmer said. "She just come back after four years of agricultural college. I don't want you running off with her."

This monument to General William Tecumseh Sherman, the great Civil War leader, reflects the gratitude of Americans for a man of firm nonathletic principles. Asked to stand for public office, Sherman made the ringing declaration, "If nominated I will not run, if elected I will not serve," thus espousing the ideals of both non-running and non-tennis. The statue, located in New York City off Central Park, portrays Sherman entering Atlanta bearing his ever-present pet pigeons, Oswaldo and Maurice, and preceded by his angelic secretary, Mrs. Vera Osmowsky, who is shown exhorting Southerners to stop running or be shot.

"Sir," said the salesman, "the last thing on my mind is running."

It's a story we tell often.

23

Distinguished Non-Runners of History

DIAMOND JIM BRADY

Immensely wealthy, Brady was also known and respected as one of the top gluttons of all time. He often ate four sheep at a single sitting, but was never once known to run a step, except toward the men's room.

JOSEF STALIN

Tyrannical dictator who ruled the Soviet Union from 1924 to 1953. Stalin considered running subversive and anti-revolutionary, since it could be employed to transport people out of the country. He often had runners shot on sight.

SOCRATES

The great philosopher had experimented with running in his youth but found that his toga got in the way, causing frequent spills. He concluded that running was not the act of an enlightened person and insisted in all his subsequent teaching

*Ancient Greek non-runners deride a passing sprinter by hurling
Frisbees and water jugs at him in this Greek drawing. Rivalry
between the two factions was intense even then.*

Toland B. Pell, Jr., of Tuscaloosa, who lost the use of both hands when struck by lightning in a 1964 marathon and vowed to convert to non-running, reads newspaper report of his winning 1978 Non-Runner of the Year Award.

that students remain seated during lessons, a tradition which continues to the present day.

PASQUALE NOWICKI

Great city planner, and a dedicated non-runner, Nowicki was years ahead of his time in his thinking. Invited in 1791 to design Washington, D.C., Nowicki, forseeing the huge traffic jams that would cripple future urban centers, laid his brilliant plans for a city entirely without streets. Unfortunately, they were rejected, but his concepts inspired generations of planners.

24

A Canadian Non-Runner Looks Back

Elmo Brack, Canadian marathon non-running champ, is well known in his country, although only among elk. In this poignant chapter from his autobiography, Non-Running to Glory, *Mr. Brack recounts his colorful childhood in Saskatoon and the day he became a non-runner:*

I learned the fine points of napping from a mysterious Occidental swami many years ago. Well, actually, it was my father. I only think of him as a mysterious swami because he never said very much. Maybe the turban had something to do with it too. But anyway, he was a master of non-running and I think that he must surely have attained the highest circle of naphood.

I remember when I was little and the exciting time would come. It was right after supper. He would look at me in that

Stunned spectators look on in helpless horror as leaders in 1973 Rio-to-São Paulo Marathon are engulfed by angry cloud of killer bees.

Non-skiers ride lift up Mount Piebald in Utah's Great Smoggy Range for an afternoon of invigorating fun. In non-skiing, America's fastest-spreading winter sport, participants arrive at mountain peak, notice they feel chilly, and take lift back to chalet for hot drink.

sublimely enlightened way of his, as if to say, "Watch this one, son," and I knew we were off to strange regions of the mind.

Then he would kind of lean backward on the couch (he was never off the couch for long—I felt it must hold some powerful totemic significance for him that I was too young to fathom) and close his eyes, the signal that the serious phase of the nap had begun. In utter fascination, I would watch his mouth drop open, realizing with mounting excitement that the snoring would soon be upon us. This was always my favorite part, that eerie rhythmic sawing (so close to the elemental flux of the ocean waves), the only time you could hear an adult speak with his nose.

I would watch transfixed, sometimes for hours, until the climax of the spectacle, that moment when my mother would enter the room and intone the ritual phrase, "Max, if you sleep any more, you'll be up all night." This would bring bravura snorts and splutters, which meant the trancelike state was over and Pop had popped back into consciousness.

For a long time, I didn't know that this drama was called napping, because my father always referred to it as "catching forty winks." This was very confusing. As closely as I watched, I never caught him winking even once. But eventually I came to understand that he was a hard-core nap freak.

25

Advanced Non-Running in Dangerous Environments

UNDERWATER

Underwater non-running is preferred by those who wish to non-run in a cool, quiet, wet environment. It can be performed in scuba gear, with snorkel, or without any equipment, provided you can find a way to breathe. It should be remembered that drowning is not a non-running activity, but floating is; so once a drowned body returns to the surface, it is technically considered to be non-running. One advantage of underwater non-running is that it may be performed among fish, one of nature's greatest natural non-runners.

DESERT

The combination of abundant sand, intense heat, and low humidity make the desert an inviting non-running arena. The sand is an effective deterrent to running. Runners go into the desert and are never seen again. Non-runners burrow in and feel at home. At night, into your tent they creep. Unlike underwater non-runners, desert non-runners should bring their water with them. It is possible, even necessary, to drink water and non-run simultaneously. Suntan lotion is a must.

JUNGLE

Jungle non-running is recommended only for the hardy, the bold, and mainly the criminally insane. This is a hostile environment for the non-runner. Everything else out there is running, most of it straight toward you. And with big teeth. The pitfalls and traps are many, the rewards few. Thus the persevering jungle non-runner deserves our admiration and in most cases, our condolences.

SPACE

Outer-space non-running is today largely a dream; but soon it will be a reality. NASA's planned Space Motel, projected for a 1986 launch, represents an ambitious effort to bring American-style non-running to the far reaches of the universe. Scientists now believe that Jupiter's atmosphere may support certain forms of non-running, and Saturn has a nice ring to it as well. Uranus is a total waste. The growing Soviet capability to blast laser rays across space and destroy hardware is not viewed as an immediate threat to non-runners, but the Intergalactic Non-Running Federation is monitoring the situation. Do we believe in Unidentified Non-Running Objects? Hell, we're still trying to figure out if there's a tooth fairy or not. Give us a break.

ARCTIC-ANTARCTIC

Ice non-running is a popular activity in the polar regions. In this event, the non-runner pours water over himself and sits on a glacier. Soon he finds himself encased in an ice block. Thousands of years later he may be found perfectly preserved by excited scientists. Or he may not. It's hard to predict. Less rigorous forms of polar non-running have been practiced by Eskimos and Laplanders for centuries, usually indoors where they can't be seen. Commodore F. Scott Persky, first non-runner to ignore the South Pole, harnessed twelve penguins to a team of huskies and sent them racing at top speed for the Pole. He stayed at base camp, enjoying innumerable bowls of hot steaming broth laced with rum.

MOUNTAIN

Mountain non-running has gained popularity ever since the invention of the helicopter. Wealthy non-runners use them to attain lofty peaks and later for the descent. Previously one had to be carried up either by animal or native guide, a tedious process which could cause you to attain lofty pique. Enormous satisfaction is gained from sitting atop an Alpine or Himalayan summit enjoying the scenic grandeur, then returning to lodge or hotel for a libation.

"Why do you not climb that mountain?" was the query put to the distinguished Alpine non-runner Sir Edmond Hilarity, which produced the classic reply, "Because I am sitting here."

Mountain non-runners should avoid the monsoon season, avalanche zones, and—at all costs—skiing.

26

Where I Non-Run

BY CELEBRITY NON-RUNNERS

ZSA ZSA GABOR

Vhenever I'm in Beverly Hills, dahlinks, vhich is vhere I am most of the time, since I live there, I like to non-run over the nehked bodies of sixteen-year-old boys vhile scattering tulip petals and singing Offenbach. This I do in the privacy of my own front lawn, so that the tourists can see it only by using binoculars.

BOB DYLAN

Here I am stuck inside Mobile with the Memphis Blues again. I ain't goin' nowhere. I'm just watchin' the river flow. No runnin' for me, man. Oo-ee, we gonna fly down into the easy chair. Yep, time passes slowly up here in the mountains.

MARSHAL TITO

I've got this neat little villa in Dubrovnik that I slip away to now and then—you know, just five or six bodyguards, my private secretary and masseuse. We get there and pull down all the shades and you know what we do? Nothing. That's right. Everyone thinks Tito's in Belgrade running the country. But you know what? I ain't running at all. So what? I can do whatever I damn please.

ANDY WARHOL

I do my non-running at Studio 54. Also my non-dancing. I just watch the others dance. Once I asked Bianca to dance with me. She said, "Oh, Andy, you're such a poor, sexless, clutzy fish. Bug off." I snapped her picture with my Instamatic as she danced off with Halston. She's a very nice girl, you know. Another time I asked Margaret Trudeau to dance. She just laughed in my face and discoed off with Mick Jagger. It's just as well. I don't really like to dance, anyway. What I really like is taking my snapshots.

ROY ROGERS

These days, most of my non-running is non-riding. You probably know by now about how I've got Trigger stuffed and mounted in the basement. Well, I like to get up there in the saddle and yell "Giddap!" and pretend we're going hell for leather like the old days. I fire off blanks too, unless Dale's home, 'cause if she is she'll come stormin' down and start in on me. So most of the time I have to be non-gunnin'. Once in a while, I like to be the Lone Ranger, just for variety. But mostly I'm just ole Roy.

MAE WEST

Run? I don't *have* to run, big boy. The men, they run after me. I sorta give a little shimmy or just lie around on my chaise lounge in a little black satin something-or-other and pretty soon they all come up and see me, if ya know what I mean. I spend most of my time just non-runnin', practicin' my double entendres, and thinkin' dirty. Who cares if I'm ninety-six? I still got what it takes.

JEAN-PAUL SARTRE

I've always felt non-running is more a state of mind than a physical act. Only when I am non-running am I truly free. The other day, de Beauvoir said to me, "Alors, J-P, how about running down to the charcuterie for a pound of chopped meat?" I pondered for a moment and then replied, "Run? Don't be silly, woman. I'm thinking."

LORETTA LYNN

Ah'm too busy for non-runnin' myself, bein' on the road twelve months a year. But ah intend to get straight back to it one a these days. Mah husband Jasper, he usually takes care of it for me. He's non-runnin' our hawg and sorghum ranch back in Arkansas. Or is it Tennessee? I forget. Anyway, ah do this song in mah act, "Ah'm Non-Runnin' Ma Heart Out Over You." It's real nice.

GERALD FORD

Well, when I was in office, of course, I was often charged with non-cunning. But I don't think that was fair, so I won't even bring it up. I did non-run in the Oval Office whenever I could. Its shape was conducive to non-running, you know, because if you tried to run in there you had to run in a tight circle—or oval, technically speaking—and you'd get dizzy fast. And then there was always the chance Kissinger might catch you and make fun of you. So I tended to non-run a lot. I liked to sit at the big desk and press the buttons and then watch the Secret Servicemen come running in looking alarmed.

JOHN DENVER

Non-running, far out. Every morning, me and Annie we're out there non-running in those beautiful Rockies. Talk about a natural high. Oh, wow! Heavy!

ANWAR EL-SADAT

The ancient Egyptians made important contributions to non-running, you know. Oh, yes. They built the pyramids, and no one was allowed to run up a pyramid. If you tried it, you'd fall right off. It was some secret in their construction. I like to go down inside the pyramids and sit in the royal burial chamber and commune with the ancient spirits.

ARNOLD PALMER

I non-run on the golf course. Where else? Golf is great for non-running. You ride around in a little cart and you hardly exert yourself at all. After eighteen holes I feel like I've been taking a nap. Very relaxing. You know, golf is a lot like taking the bus to Missoula.

MUHAMMAD ALI

I am the greatest non-runner there is. Allah says non-runnin' is the right thing to do, so I do it. I used to run a lot, but that was when I was younger. My legs ain't what they used to be, so now I just lean against the ropes and cover my head and let the other guy get tired. After a while the bell rings and here comes Cosell to interview me. He's a non-runner too. But man, is he ugly! I try not to look at him cause it makes me sick.

RICHARD NIXON

Do you know me? I used to be President once. But now, wherever I go I have to carry my American Express card to be recognized. I like to non-run on the beach at San Clemente. I put on my suit and tie and shoes and galoshes and get four Secret Service guys to carry me down to the beach. They walk up to their knees in the surf so I can get a good view. It's very relaxing, believe me.

IDI AMIN

Sure, I non-run. So does everyone else in Uganda. Ho, ho. If I'm doing it, they'd better be.

FRANK PERDUE

I make sure all my chickens non-run. That way they get fatter and juicier and I make more money. We tie 'em down in their little coops so they can't move, just eat and grow is all. I non-run, too. Often I like to sit down on a batch of eggs and help hatch them. It makes me feel really close to my chickens. Almost like a father hen.

THE BEACH BOYS

Do we non-run? We do non-run run de do non-run. Hell, Brian hasn't moved in six weeks. We're a little worried about him.

Non-Running and the Appendix

What are the effects of non-running on the appendix? This is a subject scientists are still debating, though less intensely than ever. Some contend that non-running leads to a lesser likelihood of appendicitis, while others say that the reverse may be true, or at least the opposite.

For many years, it was thought that the appendix had no function at all, that it was a fluke of nature, a waste of valuable space, an object which, if not buried deep inside the pelvis where we could not easily get at it, would doubtless be given away to the Salvation Army by most people.

Some scientists believed that at one time the appendix had been a gland secreting a digestive enzyme that made possible the ingestion of cellulose. This was eaten in the form of tree leaves, during the time that man was arboreal. The theory goes that once humans dropped to the ground and acquired a taste for nuts and berries and, later, hamburgers, the gland gradually became inert.

In the late forties, this view began to be questioned and

some researchers took the position that the appendix is a latent sexual organ. Several experiments were conducted at Stanford University, which ultimately led to the expulsion of four graduate students, a full professor, and a cleaning woman.

In 1963, Dr. Sven Entwhistle, a gastrophysicist at the Royal Stockholm Institute of Tummy-Related Disorders, postulated that the reason the appendix sometimes swells up, turns black, and bursts, releasing virulent poisons into the abdomen, is that it feels ignored and is exploding with rage. He referred to appendicitis as an "abdominal pout," and counseled that it could be prevented by a program of stroking the offended organ, whistling pleasant melodies to it, and telling it stories.

Dr. Entwhistle's theory proved highly controversial and he was denounced in respected medical journals. Smarting from the rebukes, Dr. Entwhistle took a long sabbatical from his research and then accepted a position at a leading university as head coach of the fencing team.

Later research has proven inconclusive, since one frustrated scientist after another turned from the appendix in disgust and went out to look for more promising organs to study. The problem is the appendix's amazing capacity to withhold any information about itself or its purpose. After a while, this lack of openness can dampen the enthusiasm of even the most doggedly dedicated scientist.

"The truth is," admits Dr. Flatus McGully, a former appendectomologist now devoting his time to teaching dolphins to speak Portuguese, "that after all these years we still don't know what the hell an appendix is for. Most of us don't even care anymore. In fact, as far as I'm concerned, you can take your appendix and stuff it."

Even so, before deserting their labs, appendix researchers did unearth a rich store of previously unknown facts about this cryptic organ. For one thing, it is not located in the chest, as was once thought. It is a thin, flexible, pencil-like structure, from one to six inches long, and it is attached to the cecum, a high-speed toll bypass off the large intestine.

Perhaps even more interesting than these data are the claims

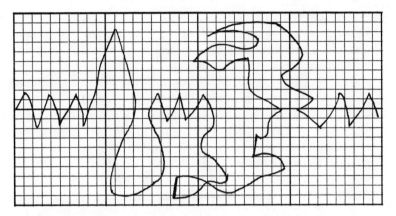

Electropendiogram shows abnormalities in the rate of chyme passage through the intestines in the appendix area, indicating likelihood of constipation attack.

that have been advanced that non-running reduces the size of the appendix. A study made in 1970 of Pakistani meter readers showed that those who habitually ran from meter to meter had 1.5 times as much appendicitis as those who sat at their desks content to let the meters come to them.

Post-mortems reveal that hot-bath takers have the tiniest appendixes, closely followed by sauna attendants. Professional hockey players and ice-show stars, on the other hand, have the largest appendixes, sometimes exceeding 2½ feet in length. This has led some scientists to theorize that cold people run the greatest risk of appendix trouble.

But, you ask, must a person give up non-running after he suffers an appendicitis attack? A generation ago this was a commonly accepted belief. But today, appendectomologists (the few left) have learned that non-running may continue after even the most vicious appendixes have been removed and destroyed.

In fact, many appendectomy victims have banded together to form medically supervised post-appendectomy napping and drinking clubs. After several years of such activity, their colonic spasm rate often drops dramatically, assuming that they also follow a regular program of eating bran flakes. Even more amazing is the fact that none of these non-runners has ever suffered a second appendectomy attack.

Still, doctors are cautious about asserting that non-running guarantees better digestion and stronger bladder control, as some non-running enthusiasts contend. It's a good thing to remember, as Dr. Theo Kazigula says in his book, *The Naked Appendix* (soon to be a TV movie starring Telly Savalas in the title role) that "a more thorough analysis of our test data is necessary before the figures can be extrapolated into a conclusion that can be accepted as anything more than encouraging."

About the Authors

Vic Ziegel and Lewis Grossberger are the pseudonyms of a pair of fabulously rich and successful sneaker manufacturers from West Germany who frankly are ashamed of the social and physical ills they have caused by conspiring to make running fashionable as a means of boosting world sneaker sales. Writing this book was their way of atoning for the damage they've done and of preventing further harm from coming to future generations.

A Note on the Type

Vic typed his stuff at forty-five words per minute. Lew typed only thirty, but took longer breaks. He's the long silent type.

This book is printed in English, a language favored by best-selling American authors, but one becoming less popular among readers. To provide contrast, an important element for reading ease, a motif of black ink on white paper was selected for the book design.